FEMINIST RESOURCES FOR SCHOOLS AND COLLEGES

FEMINIST RESOURCES FOR SCHOOLS AND COLLEGES

A Guide to Curricular Materials

Third Edition

Compiled and edited by Anne Chapman

THE FEMINIST PRESS
at The City University of New York
New York

 Published 1986
Printed in the United States of America
89 88 87 86 5 4 3 2 1

Library of Congress Cataloging in Publication Data
Chapman, Anne.
Feminist resources for schools and colleges.

Rev. and expanded ed. of: Feminist resources for schools and colleges / by Merle Froschl and Jane Williamson. 2nd ed., rev. and enl. c1977.
Includes indexes.
1. Text-books—United States—Bibliography. 2. Sex differences in education—United States—Bibliography. 3. Women's studies—United States—Bibliography. I. Froschl, Merle. Feminist resources for schools and colleges. II. Title.
Z5817.C48 1985 [LB3047] 016.3791'56'0973 85-10110
ISBN 0-935312-35-8 (pbk.)

Cover design by Lucinda Geist
Interior design by Paula J. Martinac
Typeset by Coghill Book Typesetting
Manufactured by Edwards Brothers

To my mother

CONTENTS

AUDIOVISUAL RESOURCES

PREFACE

This book is an annotated bibliography of nonsexist curricular materials for high school and undergraduate college teachers and students. First published in 1973 and now in its third edition, *Feminist Resources for Schools and Colleges* has grown into a full-sized book: the current volume is twice the size of the previous pamphlet. As the new literature and media on women grows, so grows the need for tools to select, evaluate, and access these materials.

Feminist Resources for Schools and Colleges is designed to help teachers increase their own and their students' knowledge of the new scholarship on women and to balance the traditionally male-oriented curricula through greater emphasis on women. It can be used by both beginners and those already experienced to help integrate information on women into traditional courses; to create separate courses on women; and to restructure the traditional curriculum in the light of new knowledge. It will also serve administrators in planning gender-oriented faculty development and curriculum revision projects; teacher training institutions; and librarians.

This bibliography is unique in its focus on the classroom, on teaching, and on academic subject areas—emphases not found elsewhere. Topical bibliographies on the college level are intended to serve researchers as much as, or more than, teachers. At the high school level, where teachers have less control over selection of textbook and curricular materials, there is a particular need for a guide to supplementary materials. No other current bibliography addresses gender equity in the context of the classroom and the subject matter taught.

The book is divided into two main parts: Print Resources (books, articles, pamphlets, periodicals) and Audiovisual Resources (films, filmstrips, records, cassettes, and slides). Of a total 445 entries, 310 are print resources and 135 are audiovisual resources. Within each part, entries are arranged alphabetically by author (or title, as appropriate) under academic subject areas that encompass the major disciplines in the high school and undergraduate college curriculum. Biographies, novels, poetry, and drama by individual authors are beyond the scope of this book and are not included.

Items were selected for inclusion following a thorough review of a variety of sources: standard scholarly bibliographies; reviews in relevant journals and newsletters; and catalogs of approximately 20 women's presses, 150 commercial publishers, and 50 distributors of audiovisual materials. In addition, many individuals in the field made informed and helpful suggestions. The search systematically covered materials published or produced from 1975 to 1984, when the book went into production. Thereafter, an effort was made to include significant new materials as they came to the editor's attention. Further, a few enduring works, published prior to 1975 and not superseded by more recent materials, are also included.

In considering materials for inclusion, the editor sought, though did not always find, a nonsexist outlook; a multicultural perspective; a sensitivity to issues not only of gender but of race, class, and every other form of discrimination; sound scholarship; and reader appeal. A special effort was made to find student-oriented materials; materials dealing with teaching methods; those suitable for use in high schools; and those relevant to the segments of the population most neglected in textbooks and curricula—racial and other minorities in the United States, rural, working-class, and non-Western women. Because of increasing interest by many without formal training in the new scholarship on women and gender, particular attention was paid to the needs of those new to the field.

The annotations are both descriptive and evaluative. They were designed to give readers a clear sense of the contents, approach, and style to allow them to decide whether, and how, the material will fit their needs. To some extent, the annotations also serve as immediate sources of classroom enrichment in that they often give substantive and specific information not only about the individual work but also about its subject matter. Most materials are recommended and the annotations explain why; only very exceptionally is a work included in order to caution readers against using it. In the few cases where several entries cover much the same ground, their relative merits and different uses are discussed in the annotations.

For printed material, the annotations are based on a personal check of each item and descriptions of the scope and content are frequently quoted from the text itself. Descriptions of nonprint materials are based on distributors' catalogs; a few carry quotations from reviews (consulted whenever possible in making decisions about inclusion), the source of which is identified. In addition to standard bibliographic information, where appropriate, entries provide an estimate of age level and reading level for high school audiences. (It should be noted that some materials designated for high school students can also be used with undergraduates.)

To help users find what they are looking for, author/title and subject indexes are provided, as well as a directory of publishers and distributors with ordering addresses. While all items listed were available at the time of writing (1985) from the source and at the price given in the annotation, it is recommended that readers confirm price and availability before ordering. Many publishers and distributors will send free examination copies to teachers who request them on school letterhead, stating the name of the course for which the work is being considered and the approximate enrollment. Books may also be borrowed for examination from the Department of Education's regional Sex Desegregation Assistance Centers. The address of the appropriate regional center may be obtained from the Deputy Assistant Secretary for Equal Opportunity Programs, U.S. Department of Education, 400 Maryland Avenue, S.W., Washington, D.C. 20202.

The editor hopes that readers will gain from this book, as she did from compiling it, intellectual stimulation; the challenge to stretch mentally and emotionally; and the determination to use the resources available to create a world of knowledge that includes us all.

FEMINIST RESOURCES FOR SCHOOLS AND COLLEGES

PRINT RESOURCES

BIBLIOGRAPHIES AND REFERENCE WORKS

1. Allen, Martha Leslie, ed. ***Index/Directory of Women's Media.*** Washington, D.C.: Women's Institute for Freedom of the Press. Annual. 76p. $8.00.

More than 250 U.S. and 100 international journals, newspapers, newsletters, and occasional publications of interest groups and documentation centers are featured, each with a twenty-five-word self-description. There is something here for everybody, though not anything in one convenient package specifically for the high school level. Quite specialized interests are catered to: there is the *Braille Feminist Review, La Razon Mestiza* (newsmagazine for Spanish-speaking women), the *Rural American Women News Journal, Pandora* (devoted to role-expanding science fiction), and the *Association for Women in Mathematics Newsletter.* Indexes list women's presses, publishers, and bookstores; women's music, radio, television, art, theater, and graphics groups; women's columns, speakers' bureaus, and special library collections; as well as hundreds of individual women in media, listed both alphabetically and geographically. The book's practical value will vary with individual circumstances and serendipity. A number of publications are offered free; and many publishers will send a complimentary copy to a teacher on request. Less than 50 percent overlap with **8.**

2. Bachmann, Donna G., and Piland, Sherry. ***Women Artists: An Historical, Contemporary and Feminist Bibliography.*** Metuchen, N.J.: Scarecrow Press, 1978. 353p. $20.00.

A thirteen-page introductory essay outlines issues in feminist art history and approaches to art. The bibliographical entries, most of which are annotated, are arranged into general works first, followed by materials on individual artists listed alphabetically within centuries since the fifteenth century. Entries include books, chapters and sections in books, articles, and catalogs. Each artist is introduced by a concise, informative biographical sketch, a resource in itself. Typical annotations run from a sentence to a paragraph and evaluate as well as describe the material. There are fifty-nine crisp black and white illustrations of the artists' works. A very worthwhile volume.

3. Ballou, Patricia K. ***Women: A Bibliography of Bibliographies.*** Boston: G. K. Hall, 1980. 155p. $18.00.

The 557 entries are arranged by type (including international and U.S. government documents, special periodical issues, dissertations, women's movement publications, library catalogs, guides to archives, and oral histories), by geographical area (United States and Canada, each with subdivisions; Europe, Latin America, Africa, Asia, the Middle East, and Australia/New Zealand), and by fifteen topical subject headings, including History (general, U.S., Canadian, British, European), Literature (general, U.S., Canadian, British, and other national, feminist literary criticism, children's literature and textbooks), Mass Media, Philosophy, Political Science, Anthropology (divided into general and witchcraft), Sociology (with separate sections on black, Italian, Latina, and Native American women), Psychology, Religion, Economics, Education, Fine Arts, Music, Reproduction, and Health and Sports. Publication dates of materials reviewed are mostly between 1970 and 1979. Descriptive rather than evaluative annotations of a paragraph or so give a clear idea of content and scope, often also of arrangement, and sometimes, of intent.

4. The Common Women Collective Staff. ***Women in U.S. History: An Annotated Bibliography.*** Cambridge, Mass.: The Common Women Collective, 1976. 114p. $2.60.

Includes both books and articles, and lists them under subject headings such as Anthologies; General Surveys; Historiography; Native American, Black, Pioneer, Southern White, and Institutionalized Women; Family; Social Reform; Work; and Autobiographies. Sensitive to every kind of bias, the annotations are unusually informative and outspoken; material suitable for high school use is identified. Especially good for those new to the field.

5. Frey, Linda; Frey, Marsha; and Schneider, Joanna, comps. and eds. ***Women in Western European History: A Select Chronological, Geographical, and Topical Bibliography from Antiquity to the French Revolution.*** Westport, Conn.: Greenwood Press, 1982. 760p. $49.95.

Intended for both "the scholar and the non-specialist," this massive work is "organized according to traditional time divisions." Within each division, entries are subdivided by geographical area, genre, and topic. Listed are bibliographies, surveys, biographies, and works in the political, economic, religious, social, and cultural spheres. Each of these is further subdivided; the social category, for example, into demography, family, marriage, sex life, and fashion/manners. There are nearly 7,000 entries (all of secondary sources), with separate subject and author indexes. Brief, apt quotations head each section ("Govern you then, Madame"—the Great Elector to his wife, seventeenth century Germanies, opens the politics section), an unexpected, welcome treat that could also have uses in test construction. Easy to use and valuable; a second volume is promised.

6. Green, Rayna. ***Native American Women: A Contextual Bibliography.*** Bloomington: Indiana University Press, 1983. 128p. $19.50.

A compilation of 672 alphabetically arranged entries that focuses on North America and "point[s] to decent bibliographies" for South American and U.S. Chicana women. "Material which is contained in standard ethnographies and histories" is excluded; and "materials on Native women's art, writing, traditional crafts and cuisine [are cited] only when the focus of the work [is] on the women" themselves or on their work as "women's work." Includes high school curricular materials as well as books, journal and magazine articles, theses, and audiovisual resources. One-sentence annotations are both informative and evaluative, often bluntly so: "A flimsy, unreliable narrative of Indian women and their roles in the past"; "an interesting but diversionary presentation from an utterly eccentric woman, raised by wealthy whites." The book is a gold mine of useful leads, which, however, take time to find. Despite the seventeen-page introduction (which gives a chronological review of the literature), and the period and subject index, only by reading through all the entries is it possible to locate the (numerous) items that might be useful in class. Will spark ideas.

7. Harrison, Cynthia E., ed. ***Women in American History: A Bibliography.*** Santa Barbara, Calif.: ABC-Clio, 1979. 374p. $58.00.

A guide to 3,400 articles from lesser known periodicals, publications of local and state historical societies, and professional organizations and colleges. Abstracts of 150 words or so are arranged chronologically and under each period by topics and subtopics. For example, in the period from 1783 to 1865 the topic Political Sphere has subdivisions of General, Civil War, Feminism, Abolitionism, and Utopianism; other topics include Image and Self Image; Ethnicity; and Arts and Music (including Folk Art). There are numerous articles on black and native American, some on Asian-American women. Best for those who are dedicated and/or knowledgeable.

8. ***International Guide to Women's Periodicals and Resources.*** Toronto: Resources for Feminist Research. 1981. 120p. $2.00.

Covers periodicals, journals, occasional publications, and "reference books of continuing interest to women and women's groups"; and includes listings of resource and documentation centers. There are approximately 100 Canadian entries, 250 from the United States, 150 from 13 different European countries (including some English-language materials from foreign-language countries), and a dozen or so each from Latin America, Asia, and Africa. Each annotation contains two to three sentences of self-description. Includes predominantly print resources, but is otherwise as wide-ranging as **1,** with which it has less than 50 percent overlap.

9. Katz, Elizabeth. ***Sources of Strength: Women and Culture. Annotated Bibliography.*** Newton, Mass.: Educational Development Center, 1979. 171p. $3.50.

Geared to the needs of high school teachers and students, this extensively and sensibly annotated listing of books, articles, journals, and audiovisual materials relevant to teaching and learning about African, Chinese, African-American, and Chinese-American women includes autobiography, oral history, diaries, letters, speeches, fiction (mostly by and about women), and reference works. Invaluable for its broad yet selective choice of materials, especially for student reading. Most sources were published in or before 1976; however, few are outdated, and the author has thoughtfully included a "keeping current component," listing abstracts, indexes, magazines that regularly carry reviews, and catalogs. The compiler is sensitive to issues of sex and class, politics, methodology, and multicultural perspective, and demonstrates a knowledge of student ability, maturity levels, and interests.

10. Klotman, Phyllis Rauch, and Baatz, Wilmer H., eds. ***The Black Family and the Black Woman: A Bibliography.*** Salem, N.H.: Ayer Co., 1978. 107p. $15.00.

Contains 2,000 items, some of them annotated, and arranged by subject headings. Includes history, autobiography, biography, psychology, and sociology, as well as literary works, records and tapes, government publications, and bibliographies. Approximately 200 entries describe children's materials and provide some indication of grade level. This helps to identify what might be useable in the classroom or for student assignments, as well as for teacher background.

11. Ladyslipper, Inc. ***1986 Ladyslipper Resource Guide and Catalog of Records and Tapes by Women.*** Durham, N.C.: Ladyslipper, 1986. Annual. 80p. Free.

Annotated list of several hundred items under headings including Women's and Feminist Music, Classical, Reggae, Soul, Punk, Rock, Folk and Traditional, Jazz, Blues, Children's, Spoken (Herstory and Literary), Imports and Other Languages, Budget LP's, Calendars, Postcards, and Reading Matter. Annotations are generally informative if, unsurprisingly, universally enthusiastic; most do give a good sense of content, style, and, sometimes, technical quality.

12. Loeb, Catherine. "La Chicana: A Bibliographic Survey." ***Frontiers*** 5, no. 2 (1980):59–74.

An eight-page introductory essay discusses English-language materials on Chicanas, assuming "a certain acquaintance with the issues and literature of what is commonly referred to by Chicanas as Anglo feminism." Emphasizes easily accessible recent works, but includes many hard-to-locate sources to rescue them from "their continued invisibility." Especially informative on resources about Chicana history, literature, economic and social profile, the family, and politics. Periodicals as well as articles and books are included. An alphabetical list of some 250 additional entries, without annotations, follows. Handy introduction to a badly neglected field.

13. Newton, Jennifer, and Zavits, Carol, eds. ***Women: A Bibliography of Special Periodical Issues.*** Vol. 2. Toronto: Resources for Feminist Research, 1978. 280p. $5.00.

Volume 2's completely new listing includes "only journals which are not normally concerned with women's issues," except for some "publications by established women's organizations" who have "not considered women's research a priority item"; and a "rather large number of periodicals which are not academic" but have otherwise unavailable information, interesting perspectives, or primary source materials. It provides "indices for topics which could not be categorized separately," a journal index, and an index to special publications on the male experience. Each entry lists the titles and authors of all articles included in the issue. Subject headings include Art, History, Literature, Film, Music, Mass Media, Interdisciplinary Social Sciences, and Third World Studies. For special issues published by feminist journals, see **22.**

14. Nordquist, Joan. ***Audiovisuals for Women.*** Jefferson, N.C.: McFarland, 1980. 153p. $15.95.

The 876 entries cover 16 mm. films, videotapes, filmstrips, slides, spoken word and music recordings, and contemporary filmmakers' works that are "for, about and by women produced in the English language in the U.S. and Canada." Annotations provide evaluative comments from reviews and note review sources in most instances. Especially valuable is a substantial section on "international women" from Bolivia to Canada, Vietnam to Wales, France to China. The section on "sex roles, stereotypes and discrimination" features some 20 films; "women in history: U.S.," 16 films and filmstrips; "literature," 41 spoken records under "poetry" alone. An excellent source of ideas; recommended even (or perhaps especially) for reluctant and inexperienced users of audiovisual resources.

15. Oakes, Elizabeth H., and Sheldon, Kathleen E. ***Guide to Social Science Resources in Women's Studies.*** Santa Barbara, Calif.: ABC-Clio, 1978. 162p. $24.75.

Evaluative as well as descriptive, these 654 entries with annotations of a paragraph or so often cite briefly from the work discussed. The annotations give a clear idea of what to expect: "emphasizes politics," "intensely personal and instructive," "avoids excessive economic terminology." Fascinating for the dedicated to browse through, though the reduced newsprint format is difficult to read.

16. Platt, Carolyn, and O'Neill, A. Porter, comps. ***Feminist Periodicals: A Current Listing of Contents.*** Madison: Women's Studies Librarian-at-Large, University of Wisconsin System. Quarterly. 30p. Free.

Briefly annotated alphabetical listing of some fifty major feminist journals is followed by a reproduction of tables of contents from current issues. The aim is to "keep the reader abreast of current topics in feminist literature; to increase readers' familiarity with a wide spectrum of feminist periodicals; and to provide the requisite bibliographic information should a reader wish to subscribe to a journal or obtain a particular article at her library or through interlibrary loan."

17. Sicherman, Barbara; Monter, E. William; Scott, Joan Wallach; and Sklar, Kathryn Kish. ***Recent United States Scholarship on the History of Women.*** Washington, D.C.: American Historical Association, 1980. 53p. $4.50.

In the context of a 28-page essay, 174 books and articles are reviewed. The essay discusses, fully but concisely, major issues and events in the history of women in Europe and the United States. Readable by the nonspecialist, this is among the most useful brief introductions to women's history.

18. Stineman, Esther, and Loeb, Catherine. ***Women's Studies: A Recommended Core Bibliography.*** Littleton, Colo.: Libraries Unlimited, 1979. 670p. $45.00.

Extremely valuable for the detail and quality of its annotations (even when one disagrees with them), this volume lists 1,763 books, periodicals, and other publications, almost exclusively originating in the United States. Entries, which concentrate on biography, autobiography, letters, diaries, and journals, are grouped under 25 headings. The annotations, averaging half a page, sketch not only content but the author's point of view, and how the work compares to others on the same topic. Occasionally, an annotation will expand into a discussion of the subject that goes well beyond the individual work considered; reading through the volume virtually amounts to a rapid, nontechnical, and opinionated mini-course in women's studies. There are separate author, title, and subject indexes. This is by far the most useful starting point for those with little or no background in women's studies.

19. Sullivan, Kaye. ***Films for, by and about Women.*** Metuchen, N.J.: Scarecrow Press, 1980. 560p. $27.50.

Aims to "provide a better perspective on the relationship between being human and being a woman or a man" and to "present women filmmakers and identify the source of films made by each one." Lists some 2,800 film titles (features, documentaries, and shorts) made by, or of special interest to, women; the vast majority date from before 1975, and none are included from after 1978. Descriptions of two to three sentences give a reasonably good idea of content and sometimes of format. Subject index entries include Abortion, Adolescence, Authors, Blacks, Family Life (including Alternative Lifestyles), Geographical Areas, History, Literature, Minorities, Sex Roles, Social Protest, and Women's Rights. A directory of film sources and filmmakers and a bibliography are also featured. Still useful for films made by women; much of what it features for and about women is outdated and/or superseded. Overall, **14** is a better choice.

20. Terborg-Penn, Rosalyn. "Teaching the History of Black Women: A Bibliographical Essay." ***The History Teacher*** 13, no. 2 (February 1980): 245–50.

Reviews recent books and articles and some older, classic studies; suggests topics for both chronological and thematic treatments of black women's history, and the writing relevant to each topic, whether narrative, analytical, and/or collections of original sources. Particularly useful in course planning.

21. Terris, Virginia R., ed. ***Woman in America: A Guide to Information Sources.*** Detroit: Gale, 1980. 520p. $55.00.

The nearly 2,500 entries here are arranged in 10 categories: General References; Role, Image and Status; History; the Women's Movement; Education; Sociology; Employment; Health and Sexuality; the Arts; Biography and Autobiography. Terse but informative annotations run from one to three sentences in length: "momism with a vengeance," "broad view of problems and triumphs," "discusses 30 pioneers." Terris says she "favored the more general readership" while hoping not to neglect the "skilled researcher." The book is definitely more useful to those with some knowledge about the history of and current academic concerns about women in America.

22. Walton, Whitney; Loeb, Cathy; and Stineman, Esther, comps. ***Current Sources on Women and Literature.*** Madison, Wis.: University of Wisconsin System, 1979. 52p. Free.

Lists books, articles, and special issues of periodicals and dissertations, published between 1977 and 1979, "about women authors and their writings, feminist analysis of works by both male and female authors, and works on women characters in literature by male and female authors." Focuses on critical works, excluding fiction, poetry, and drama. Titles of studies of specific female and male authors can be found through an alphabetical listing of some thirty writers including Brecht, Chopin, Flaubert, Lessing, Sappho, Trollope, Wheatley, and Yeats. The index of "Genres" lists works that deal with "types of literature or groups of works by several authors" (such as "Diary Keeping as a Feminist Art Form" or "Literary Images of Mexican-American Women"). Bibliographies and feminist literary criticism are listed under separate "Reference" and "Theory" headings. Entries are not annotated, except for the listing of special periodical issues that focus on women in literature. A useful starting place for teachers in finding feminist approaches to works in their syllabi (Shakespeare, Dickens, James, for example), and as an introduction to feminist literary theory.

23. Williamson, Jane, ed. ***New Feminist Scholarship: A Guide to Bibliographies.*** Old Westbury, N.Y.: The Feminist Press, 1979. 144p. $15.00.

Almost 400 entries, about half of them annotated, include books, journals, government documents, organizations and agencies, special interest groups, and other nonbook resources. They are arranged in thirty categories, including Anthropology, Art, Education, History, Politics, Rape and Sex Roles, Third World Countries, and Work. Annotations of a sentence to a page in length vary from the richly informative to some that are irritatingly incomplete. Good in its coverage of materials from sources other than commercial publishers.

24. Women and Literature Collective. ***Women and Literature: An Annotated Bibliography of Women Writers.*** 3d rev. ed. Cambridge, Mass.: Women and Literature Collective, 1976. 212p. $5.00.

Contains 819 entries focusing on "women's fictional writings plus other forms of expressive prose" chosen with "feminist concerns in mind." Entries are divided by countries (United States, Britain, eight European countries, Africa, Asia, Australia, Israel, Japan, Latin America, New Zealand), and by periods. Each author's works are headed by a paragraph or two of concise, pithy, and useful information about her life, work, and place in literary history—a valuable resource in itself. Entries give some idea of plot, style, characters, and feminist significance in vivid prose ("plot and prose nosedive into semi-coherent sentimentality"; "the marriage ends positively in divorce"). Many of the books reviewed are suitable for high school readers; they range from classic novels to a "feminist Western," thrillers, fantasy, experimental literature, and nonsexist childrens'/young adults' books. Separate author and subject indexes are included. A valuable source of ideas as well as information.

PERIODICALS

25. ***Catalyst Media Review.*** New York: Catalyst. Bi-monthly periodical. 10p. $12.00 for 5 issues. Annual index.

An annotated bibliography of videotapes, films, and filmstrips relating to women and work, based on monitoring the output of over 400 major producers. Sex roles, two-career families, shared parenting, working mothers, nontraditional careers, displaced homemakers, and women in management are the topics of recent works reviewed. Annotations give technical information, target audience, a synopsis, and evaluative comments, with enough detail to make possible an informed decision.

26. ***Feminist Studies.*** College Park: University of Maryland. 3 issues per year. 180p. $18.00/year.

The editors "wish not just to interpret women's experiences but to change women's conditions." The approach is inclusive; recent issues have featured poems, graphics, a historical study of child custody, accounts of black women under slavery, short stories, book reviews, literary criticism, and interviews. Over the last five years, there has been both impeccable and some shaky scholarship, schematic rhetoric, and gripping personal statement, with a recent trend toward the more academic. College level.

27. ***Journal of Family History.*** Greenwich, Conn.: JAI Press. Quarterly. $5.50/issue, $25.00/year.

Scholarly and authoritative. While many of the articles are narrowly technical or case studies of restricted scope, some could be useful to classroom teachers. Noteworthy are two recent special issues: Spring 1982, The Family in Eastern Europe, and Spring 1983, The Family in Japanese History; and the review essay on Russian historical demography and family history in the Fall 1981 issue.

28. ***On Campus with Women.*** Washington, D.C.: Association of American Colleges. Quarterly. 12p. $15.00/year.

A newsletter focusing on topics such as affirmative action, women's education and employment, sexual harassment and rape, women in sports and science, and minority women. Its reports are brief (typically a paragraph or two), pithy, intriguingly written, and crammed with information on legislation, court action, courses, research, resources, and statistics. The text is exclusively factual, offering neither opinion nor analysis; titles have ranged from "Unwed is Not Unfit," to "Sexist Therapy: It's All in the Mind," and "Math Anxiety Adds Up." *On Campus* periodically issues valuable special reports, such as "Classroom Climate: A Chilly One for Women," which outlines specific ways in which teachers consciously and unconsciously treat women and minority students differently from WASP males. Aimed at college audiences, but worthwhile for all those who like to keep informed along a broad front.

29. ***Signs: Journal of Women in Culture and Society.*** Chicago: University of Chicago Press. Quarterly. 200p. $7.00/issue, $27.50/year.

Authoritative and oriented toward international scholarship, its primary usefulness for the high school teacher lies in the regularly featured review essays surveying the state of the art in a particular subject area that run to perhaps a dozen pages. These are usually informative yet not too weighty even for the nonspecialist, and give a very good idea of current issues in the field.

30. ***TABS: Aids for Ending Sexism in School.*** Brooklyn, N.Y.: TABS. Quarterly. $8.50/year.

Focuses on classroom aids for kindergarten through 12th grade: posters, lesson plans, awareness exercises, readers' idea sharing, brief news items, and reviews. There are poems, stories, and mini-biographies for students to read, with suggestions for classroom activities based on them. Most of the material is directed at the pre-high school level, but secondary school teachers will also find some easy-to-use ideas and materials, especially for 9th and 10th graders.

31. ***Women Studies Abstracts.*** Rush, N.Y.: Rush Publishing. Quarterly. $36.00/year.

Lists over 2,500 articles annually from a wide range of publications, identifying contents of special journal issues. Abstracts are very brief and accompany a minority of the entries. Also mentioned are new books, with information on where these have been reviewed. Entries are arranged under 18 headings, including Literature, Art, Media Reviews, Biography, History, and Criticism. Useful for those with an instinct for what might be of interest and a willingness to investigate further.

32. ***Women's Studies International Forum.*** Elmsford, N.Y.: Pergamon Press. Bimonthly. About 200 pages. $30.00/year.

This is a "multidisciplinary journal for the rapid publication of research communications and review articles in women's studies." Its aim is to "critique and reconceptualize existing knowledge, and to examine, and reevaluate the manner in which knowledge is produced and distributed, and the implications this has for women's position." Contributors are those engaged in feminist research "inside or outside formal educational institutions"; and articles include the action-oriented as well as the theoretical, the methodological, and case-studies. The journal also publishes review articles, book reviews, symposia, and announcements. Serves to keep teachers abreast of cutting-edge developments.

33. ***Women's Studies Quarterly.*** New York: The Feminist Press at The City University of New York. Quarterly. 48p. $25.00/year.

This is a "must" for keeping up with what is going on in women's studies at all educational levels (high school-related material has appeared in virtually every issue) and in surprisingly varied community and institutional settings, primarily in the United States but with some international coverage. It includes announcements and reports on courses, conferences, organizations, and publications. Includes descriptive lists of Women's Studies Programs and the Centers of the National Council for Research on Women, updated annually.

INTERDISCIPLINARY APPROACHES

WOMEN'S STUDIES

Theory and Philosophy

34. Agonito, Rosemary, ed. ***History of Ideas on Woman: A Source Book.*** New York: Putnam, 1977. 414p. $5.95.

These thirty selections, four by women, from Aristotle through Bacon, Kirkegaard, Horney, Marcuse, and Friedan, are chosen "because of their influence" and because they are "representative of [the issues and the thinking of] their various periods." Clear, concise, readable, and very informative headnotes of a page or so give some historical context for each selection, summarize the ideas in it, and comment on their significance. An appendix gives biographical notes on each author. Students could be assigned the headnotes only, which competent readers would have little trouble with; most of the selections take dedication to wade through.

35. Bowles, Gloria, and Klein, Renate Duelli, eds. ***Theories of Women's Studies.*** Boston: Routledge & Kegan Paul, 1983. 277p. $8.95.

Thirteen papers in this collection written between 1979 and 1982 "ask questions about the nature of Women's Studies in higher education and . . . how Women's Studies as a discipline is different in content, in form, in aims and objectives from the traditional disciplines." The editors' introduction sets the contributions in the framework of what they see as "that crucial debate which will shape the development of Women's Studies throughout the 1980s": the relationship of Women's Studies as a separate entity to those efforts to integrate it into the disciplines. The essays range from a consideration of "values, knowing and method in feminist social science" to quantitative methodology, experiential analysis, feminism and the humanities, and the learning experience in women's studies. The book includes a thirty-six-page "selected annotated bibliography of articles on theories of Women's Studies."

36. Boxer, Marilyn J. "Review Essay: For and about Women: The Theory and Practice of Women's Studies in the United States." ***Signs*** 7, no. 3 (Spring 1982): 661–95.

Surveys "the literature about women's studies as a field in American higher education: its history, political issues, theories and structures," most of which has appeared in periodicals. The "symbiotic relationship between women's studies and women's liberation" is seen as the former's greatest promise and most enduring problem.

37. Clark, Lorenne M. G., and Lange, Lynda, eds. ***The Sexism of Social and Political Theory: Women and Reproduction from Plato to Nietzsche.*** Buffalo: University of Toronto Press, 1979. 141p. $7.95.

Ten- to twenty-page essays, filled with quotations from their subjects, examine the assumptions of seven philosophers about women's "nature" and sex roles; and show how their exclusion of women from the political sphere is related to other basic ideas of the philosophers considered. With perseverance, most of the essays are readable by the nonspecialist.

38. Daly, Mary. ***Gyn/Ecology: The Metaethics of Radical Feminism.*** Boston: Beacon Press, 1979. 485p. $9.95.

According to the author, "this is an extremist book." It is "about the journey of women becoming, that is, radical feminism," which "involves exorcism of the internalized Godfather." Affirming that "everything is connected," the author's rhetorical, punning, alliterative, incantatory writing ranges over a reinterpretation of patriarchal (primarily Christian) myth (transformation of the "tree of life" to the "torture cross," the wine at the Eucharist as a "version of Male Menstruation"); analysis of Indian *suttee,* Chinese footbinding, African genital mutilation, European witchburnings, and American gynecology as "woman-hating rituals" of the patriarchy, whose ultimate intent is to "castrate, that is, to deprive women of vigor, vitality, and finally life itself"; and a celebration of the empowerment to be had from the transformation of language, from female friendship and spinning the thread of connection, and from the freeing of the self from fears. Exuberance in wordplay (controlled by careful "attention to etymology, to varied dimensions of meaning and subliminal associations") is at the service of a combative intelligence that scathingly denounces the "malevolence of male violence" and the "necrophilic leaders of phallotechnic society." Requires careful reading.

39. Driver, Anne Barstow. "Review Essay: Religion." ***Signs*** 2, no. 2 (Winter 1976): 434–42.

The focus is on Christian writers' critiques of religious tradition as "our most deep-seated cause of patriarchy," and exploration of "new religious formulas" that might overcome sexism.

40. Elshtain, Jean Bethke. ***Public Man, Private Woman: Women in Social and Political Thought.*** Princeton: Princeton University Press, 1981. 376p. $8.95.

Aware that her ideas—as those of the thinkers she discusses—"might have effects on real people," the author links notions of public and private to "understandings of human nature, theories of language and action, and the divergent values and ends of familial and political life." She examines the connections among an "august array of thinkers . . . representative of the Western political tradition": Plato, the Christian theorists, Rousseau, Hegel, Marx, and Mill; and gives a somewhat controversial summary, with critique, of contemporary radical, liberal, Marxist, and psychoanalytic feminism. The occasionally colorful prose (e.g., "labeling both [Mbuti and U.S. society] patriarchal is rather like trying to derive an elephant from an earthworm") makes for stimulating reading for interested teachers. The sixteen-page bibliography offers some interesting leads.

41. English, Jane. "Review Essay: Philosophy." ***Signs*** 3, no. 4 (Summer 1978): 823–31.

Outlines the work of feminist philosophers in the areas of moral issues, political theories, sexism in scientific methodology and assumptions, linguistic arguments, and metaphysical issues.

42. Jaggar, Alison M., and Struhl, Paula Rothenberg. ***Feminist Frameworks: Alternative Theoretical Accounts of the Relations between Women and Men.*** New York: McGraw-Hill, 1984. 2d ed. 446p. $18.95.

The authors provide fourteen readings by people of different sexes, ages, and ethnic backgrounds to "show how contemporary social arrangements . . . fail to promote personal happiness and fulfillment," focusing on problems in the areas of work, the family, and sexuality. Next, they present selections from "classic statements by major proponents" of conservative, liberal, traditional Marxist, radical feminist, and social feminist theories. Finally, the authors apply the theoretical frameworks to the three problem areas, with two readings for each theoretical orientation in each area. Promotes a sound grasp of the theories discussed; some of it would be readable by competent, mature high school students.

43. Langland, Elizabeth, and Gove, Walter, eds. ***A Feminist Perspective in the Academy: The Difference It Makes.*** Chicago: University of Chicago Press, 1981. 168p. $5.95.

Nine essays by well-known scholars review new feminist scholarship and its real and potential impact on the critical study of literature, the performing arts, religion, history, political science, economics, anthropology, psychology, and sociology. The essays summarize new information and new points of view, and suggest in some detail where and how these could and should be used in learning and teaching. They also make clear that what they speak of is not "additional knowledge merely to be tacked on to the curriculum. It is, instead, . . . perspective transforming [and] fundamental to the development and vitality of every discipline." Authoritative yet nontechnical, and reasonably easy to read even for those with no background in the disciplines discussed.

44. Mahowald, Mary Briody, ed. ***Philosophy of Woman: An Anthology of Classic and Current Concepts.*** 2d ed. Indianapolis: Hackett, 1983. 480p. $8.50.

These thirty-six selections, fifteen of them by women, are grouped to treat first the "extant popular concepts" of womanhood, both feminist and antifeminist. They then look at "the available philosophical approaches to the meaning of woman in contemporary society": utilitarian, existential, Marxist, and analytic, and "project what prominent philosophers of the past had to say," followed by the contributions of psychoanalytic theory. Last, "the present stage of philosophical inquiry" is discussed. Headnotes give biographical information, and identify as well as comment on the major issues raised; they are less suitable to stand on their own than are those in **34.** Most of the selections are difficult to read; some, especially if edited, could be tackled by able 12th graders. The broad selection and contemporary emphasis are a plus; each section lists "related readings" with a feminist perspective.

45. McAllister, Pam, ed. ***Reweaving the Web of Life: Feminism and Non-Violence.*** Philadelphia: New Society, 1982. 448p. $8.95.

An anthology of poems, interviews, essays, artwork, memoirs, photos, letters, and fiction by over fifty contributors who differ widely in age, race, ethnicity, and class background. The first, primarily theoretical, part offers essays such as "Fear of 'Other': The Common Root of Sexism and Militarism," "The Economic Roots of the Violent Male Culture," and " 'Free Speech' and Black Struggle." The second part shows how a feminist perspective on nonviolence has been applied to antiwar, antinuclear, and antiracism work, self-defense, personal relationships, abortion, and more. It is, in turn, outspoken, raw, harrowing, outraged, energetic, naive, disorganized, provocative, repetitive, unfocused, and interesting. Includes a five-page annotated bibliography and a chronology of events referred to since 1600. Some excerpts could be assigned to some students.

46. McLure, Gail Thomas, and McLure, John W. ***Women's Studies.*** Washington, D.C.: National Education Association, 1977. 80p. $5.95.

Designed to "help educators decide what women's studies should consist of in their school systems," this booklet is more useful in legitimizing women's studies than in helping teachers implement it at the secondary level. The authors see sex-role stereotyping as the "problem to which women's studies is part of the solution," and they consider "a major long-term goal of women's studies as a separate topic" to be the creation of its "own obsolescence." The authors give a brief account of the theory and practice of sex-role development and discuss some ways to promote psychological androgyny. Direct and indirect approaches to integrating women's studies into the K–12 curriculum are briefly discussed by subject area: reading and language arts, social studies, math, science, fine arts, foreign languages, and other areas of school life, such as sports and counseling. The references given will not be helpful for those seeking greater depth. A starting point.

47. Oakley, Ann. ***Subject Women.*** New York: Pantheon, 1981. 406p. $7.95.

Under headings of Citizenship, The Making of a Woman, Labour, Relationships, Power, and A Subject Gender, this book deals with a wide range of topics. The author writes on the effects of X and Y chromosomes on health and mortality, "female-male relations as a defining feature of femininity in the modern world," "poverty [as] a special trap for women," preconceptions about housework, and the various flavors of feminism. Including mostly British and American, with some European and non-Western material, and drawn from a wide range of disciplines, this sprawling work sports a great many quotations from authorities and primary sources in the various fields, as well as dozens of statistical tables amidst a vigorous, flowing, scholarly text. Strong organization counteracts the tendency toward a smorgasbord effect. The fifty-page bibliography is wide-ranging, idiosyncratic, and leans towards the technical. Some of the quotations and tables could be assigned to students of varying reading abilities, or used in the classroom. (For suggestions on using statistics in the classroom, see **196.**)

48. Osborne, Martha Lee. ***Genuine Risk: A Dialogue on Woman.*** Indianapolis: Hackett, 1981. 78p. $2.50.

A lively, witty, and smooth-flowing conversation between a sexist male and two female students, one of them a militant feminist. The dialogue highlights in dramatic form arguments concerning woman's "physical, mental and moral capacities; the value of her contributions to science, religion and the arts; the validity of her claims to preferential treatment in the job market"; and her relationship to husband and children within the family. Not all of the arguments "are sound; not all are even effective—but all are familiar. It is hoped that a careful assessment of each of them will stimulate the reader to make an informed, independent and valid judgement" on these matters. Designed as three assignments, each includes six to twelve mind-stretching discussion questions for students. For teachers who have some acquaintance with current research and thinking on the topics introduced, assigning this book to students is an excellent way to promote discussion of issues covered. Accessible to average 11th and 12th grade readers.

49. Osborne, Martha Lee. ***Woman in Western Thought.*** New York: Random House, 1978. 341p. $12.00.

Selections from twenty authors, including Plato, Spinoza, Kant, Sarah Grimké, Hegel, Fuller, Sartre, and De Beauvoir. Each selection is headed by a note outlining the author's life, historical setting, and other theories, which could usefully be read by students. A response to, or further exploration of, the ideas presented in the excerpt follows each, written by a modern or contemporary commentator. Selections are arranged chronologically, and are cross-referenced by ten topics, including women and work, education, religion, morality, and the state. Somewhat formidable, but stimulating; occasional technical vocabulary is not a ban to understanding by the nonexpert. Selectively assignable to able, mature students.

50. Radcliffe, Janet Richards. ***The Sceptical Feminist: A Philosophical Enquiry.*** Boston: Routledge & Kegan Paul, 1980. 308p. $9.50.

"Feminism is not concerned with a group of people it wants to benefit, but with a type of injustice it wants to eliminate." In this clear-headed, closely reasoned, and balanced study the author considers such issues as "the elements of irrationality in feminism," the relevance of arguments about women's "nature," freedom and conditioning, feminism and femininity, women's work and their control over their bodies, and the importance of feminism relative to other moral issues. Avoiding both speculation and polemic, the author provides an overview of major concerns, strengths, and weaknesses, and a flavor of a significant segment of the contemporary feminist movement. Lucid prose, logical argument, and judicious selection of illustrative examples in the service of a controversial (because seen by some as a one-sidedly "liberal") stance.

51. Sherman, Julia A., and Beck, Evelyn Torton, eds. ***The Prism of Sex: Essays in the Sociology of Knowledge.*** Madison: University of Wisconsin Press, 1979. 320p. $19.50.

Nine essays in history, literature, political science, psychology, sociology, and philosophy by established and up-and-coming scholars who critique their fields for "patriarchal bias" and "challenge the very foundations on which the state of knowledge in each discipline is grounded." A resource that is best, perhaps, for introducing those who are already aware in their own field to the state of the art in others. Essays on United States and European history are relatively more accessible to general readers than the rest.

52. Spender, Dale, ed. ***Men's Studies Modified: The Impact of Feminism on the Academic Disciplines.*** New York: Pergamon Press, 1981. 350p. $14.50.

Fifteen essays by American, Australian, and British scholars and feminists show "what men left out in the codification of knowledge" and how, by including women, "feminists have transformed not just the knowledge itself but the processes whereby knowledge is produced." The subject areas discussed are language, literary criticism, history (both United States and European), media studies, education, medicine, biology, and the scientific ethic. "Two issues which arise [repeatedly in the various essays and] which seem to be fundamental" are "the polarized and discrete categories of objectivity/subjectivity," and the "linguistic issue, the use of the term *man*." With varying degrees of thoroughness, contributors review feminist books and articles in their subject area, providing a useful overview of new information and ideas. Several also consider the status of women within the institutions of their discipline; and some deal with the most basic issue—the debate, initiated by feminist questioning, concerning acceptable criteria of scholarship in any discipline. For those new to the field it is best read after **43**, in comparison with which it is more technical and less accessible.

Anthologies and Texts

53. Freeman, Jo. ***Women: A Feminist Perspective.*** 3d ed. Palo Alto, Calif.: Mayfield, 1984. 621p. $15.95.

Thirty-two essays, many by authorities in their field, contain "information that cannot easily be found anywhere else." The book provides a comprehensive and somewhat dense introduction to middle-of-the-road feminist thought on the body and its control, the family, growing up, work, institutions of social control, and feminism itself. Contributors cover such varied topics as the population explosion, rape and abortion, power in dating relationships, clerical and professional work, women's labor history, why witches were women, sexism and language, legal issues, black women, and male power and the women's movement. A teacher's resource, it is substantial and thought-provoking.

54. Goddard-Cambridge Graduate Program in Social Change. ***Breaking the Silence: Seven Courses in Women's Studies.*** Newton, Mass.: Educational Development Center, 1980. 166p. $7.25.

The units on "Reading and Writing About Women's Lives" and "Black Women Writers" suggest readings (and ways to discuss them) that speak powerfully to students as they teach literary skills. The "short and basic" women's history unit, supplemented by an annotated resource list, is unusual in its concentration on the experience of "neglected" (Third World, ethnic, and working-class) women. Units on sex roles and work provide useful information on practical issues. Overall, while the book generates ideas and suggests some ways of putting them into practice, it is somewhat sketchy. Those new to the field especially should use it only in conjunction with more extensive treatments of the topics covered.

55. Hull, Gloria T.; Scott, Patricia Bell; and Smith, Barbara, eds. ***All the Women Are White, All the Blacks Are Men, But Some of Us Are Brave: Black Women's Studies.*** Old Westbury, N.Y.: The Feminist Press, 1981. 420p. $12.95.

Written with a view toward the "necessity for Black women's studies to be feminist, radical and analytical," this book "illuminates and provides examples of recent research and teaching about Black women." It is "a reference text and pedagogical tool," providing substantive information and suggestions on a number of topics, including teaching about the black female slave, and studying black women writers. It also gives a critique of black women's treatment by the social sciences, and guidelines on consciousness raising about racism. Many of the specific ideas and approaches could be adapted for the high school classroom. Contains six useful bibliographic essays on black women in history, literature, and music; an eighteen-page, partially annotated listing of nonprint materials; and twenty detailed course syllabi.

56. Hunter College Women's Studies Collective. ***Women's Realities, Women's Choices: An Introduction to Women's Studies.*** New York: Oxford University Press, 1983. 621p. $14.95.

A "basic textbook written for introductory women's studies courses," and "thoroughly interdisciplinary," this sprawling work tries to be all things to all women. It deals with imagery and symbolism in the definition of women; women's "nature"; women's bodies, personalities, and social roles; women's family relationships as daughters, sisters, wives, mothers, and in alternative living arrangements (utopian, communal, and single); and women in society, through aspects of religion, education, health, work, political power, and social change. Over eighty brief readings, from a couple of paragraphs to a page or so, include a poem by Sappho, guidelines for questions to ask of a "health care practitioner," the time allocation for various rural activities, Nietzsche on women, *marianisma* as part of Chicana socialization, and a contemporary "invocation to the Goddess." Each chapter concludes with a number of sensible (rather than inspiring) discussion questions, an annotated group of recommended readings, and a list of references. The narrative format complements the more document-oriented one of **60;** both should be considered in the teaching or planning of a women's studies course. Note that much the same subject matter is covered in **122, 307,** and **308.**

57. McRobbie, Angela, and McCabe, Trisha, eds. ***Feminism for Girls: An Adventure Story.*** Boston: Routledge & Kegan Paul, 1981. 256p. $11.50.

The first feminist book in Britain written especially for teenagers and somewhat expensively available in the United States, this unfortunately cannot be recommended—less because of the fairly substantial amount of material that is too specifically British to be useful than because of its lack of focus and weak content. Seventeen chapters by different contributors offer a hodge-podge ranging from a description of different classroom expectations for the two sexes to an indifferent short story by a 16-year-old about going to a disco. Other chapters discuss the economic and psychological realities of being a secretary, and sex in advertising (for a better source see **148**). Also included: interviews with young marrieds on how it feels to be a wife and mother, and a "note on Lesbian sexuality." The individual selections as well as the book as a whole are disappointing. The information-oriented chapters lack hard data and incisive thinking; the personal experience narratives lack direction and emphasis.

58. Mitchell, Joyce Slayton, ed. ***Other Choices for Becoming a Woman: A Handbook to Help High School Women Make Decisions.*** Rev. ed. Pittsburgh, Penn.: Know Inc., 1975. 267p. $6.00.

Shallow discussions from eleven contributors on making sexual, social, marital, fashion, drug, religious, and educational choices. The result is largely bland conventional wisdom; all sensitive issues such as those concerning sexism, class, race, and sexual orientation are ignored. Some of the material is out of date.

59. Morgan, Robin, ed. ***Sisterhood Is Powerful: An Anthology of Writings from the Women's Liberation Movement.*** New York: Random House, 1970. 648p. $12.95.

A classic that continues to be of more than historical interest. Coverage includes women's work, psychology, sexuality, and image; women and aging; the welfare system and the church; black, Chicana, lesbian, and high school women; poems, manifestos, articles; and detached and outraged voices dealing with many facets of contemporary women's lives. Readings vary in difficulty; many are accessible to adequate readers, 10th grade and up. However, teachers need some grounding in women's studies before attempting to use this book with students.

60. Ruth, Sheila. ***Issues in Feminism: A First Course in Women's Studies.*** Boston: Houghton Mifflin, 1980. 593p. $17.50.

This lucid, passionate, and analytical book, "designed for beginners," brings together "statements, judgements and arguments from past and present that . . . have had terrific impact on the lives of women (and hence of men) and still do." A seventeen-page introduction traces the connections of women's studies with feminism, counters the charge that women's studies is a biased discipline, and outlines "the terms and techniques" of women's studies and its position in academe. In its first five chapters, the book explores consciousness—the meanings, expectations, and images that form "the 'head-set' of sexual reality." It examines the "masculinist society in which we live," patriarchal stereotypes and feminist images of women, and theories about the "asymmetry" between the sexes. Three more chapters deal with "the outward realization of sexist consciousness" by looking at the spheres of personal relationships as lived and perceived, as well as the institutional spheres of work, law, and politics. In each chapter, the author explains and illustrates terminology, concepts, and points of view, and comments on them as an individual, a philosopher, and a feminist. Each chapter is accompanied by readings of one to twelve pages, totalling some fifty readings altogether. Authors of readings range from the widely known (Aquinas and De Beauvoir, Tiger and Millett) to those less well known; and cover issues from the psychology of rape to women and social security, from "wiving" to racism and sexism. Brief notes to each section give biographical information and pinpoint main ideas. A twelve-page "Chronology Highlighting Women's History in the United States" and a nineteen-page bibliography are included. Although perhaps too ambitious in scope for the absolute beginner, this book is nevertheless the clearest and most thorough one-volume survey of women's studies. Some of the readings can be assigned to competent or better readers, 10th grade and up.

61. Spretnak, Charlene, ed. ***The Politics of Women's Spirituality: Essays on the Rise of Spiritual Power within the Feminist Movement.*** Garden City, N.Y.: Doubleday, 1982. 624p. $12.95.

"All the pieces in this anthology [nearly half of them new, many of the rest often considered feminist classics] are active rather than reactive, are revolutionary rather than reformist, and express broad political awareness." Forty-six contributors from various religious, racial, and ethnic backgrounds include Broner, Chesler, Chicago,

Daly, Rich, Shange, Starhawk, Steinem, and Stone. Their topics range from "Women and Culture in Goddess-Oriented Old Europe" to "Consciousness, Politics and Magic," "Contemporary Feminist Rituals," "Martial Arts Meditations," "WITCH: Spooking the Patriarchy during the Late Sixties," "Spiritual Techniques for Re-Powering Survivors of Sexual Assault," and "The Christian Right's 'Holy War' against Feminism." Selections speak in many voices: scholarly, militant, lyrical, and, overwhelmingly, radical. Those to whom the orientation of contributors and their basic concepts are new will gain an understanding of this aspect of feminist thought and feeling by reading widely, and openmindedly, in this book.

Women's Movement and Women's Rights

62. Altbach, Edith Hoshino, ed. ***From Feminism to Liberation.*** Rev. ed. Cambridge, Mass.: Schenkman, 1980. 328p. $8.95.

This collection of twenty-five documents, articles, and poems from the 1960s and 1970s presents the theory and history of the twentieth-century women's liberation movement and its connections with civil rights, the new Left, and socialism. It includes pieces on housework, the ideology of the family, racism, psychology's construction of the female, women as producers, abortion, class, and culture. While the final essay helps to provide a context, the book is aimed at an audience already acquainted with the subject area.

63. Gordon, Linda. ***Woman's Body, Woman's Right: Birth Control in America.*** New York: Penguin, 1977. 479p. $7.95.

Everything you are likely to want to know about the subject, treated very broadly in the context of ideological, economic, and social change. The focus is on "women seeking sexual and reproductive self-determination"; the book deals with the ideas, constituency, motivations, and needs both of the movement's advocates and its opponents "from the mid-19th century, when feminists attacked unwanted pregnancies in the name of sacred female chastity, to the 20th century, when contraception has been blamed for a breakdown in the traditional standards of chastity." The scene is set by a discussion of birth control (as practiced in all its modern forms, including abortion, but excluding the pill) in traditional societies. The analysis treats issues of class and race. Scholarly but readable by the nonspecialist, the text includes quotations from primary sources. Those interested only in birth control will have to wade through a considerable volume of information on other topics; the book is enriching but time-consuming.

64. Nicholas, Susan Cary; Price, Alice M.; and Rubin, Rachel. 2d ed. ***Rights and Wrongs: Women's Struggle for Legal Equality.*** New York: The Feminist Press at The City University of New York, 1986. 112 pp. $7.95.

This compact narrative gives an account of legal issues in "four major areas of concern to women—constitutional law, the family, employment, and the right to control their own bodies." It provides a clear, succinct overview of the U.S. legal system; a history of the equal rights struggle and of traditional marriage as a legal agreement; examples of experiments in redefining marriage; an account of protective and antidiscrimination legislation in employment and affirmative action; and a discussion of legal aspects of rape, abortion, and contraception. The plain prose is varied with excerpts of a paragraph to a page or more from trials, court opinions, contracts, and other documents. For competent 10th grade readers and up. The *Teaching Guide* by Neale McGoldrick (47p., $4.00) gives ideas for using the text in formats ranging from four to five classroom meetings to six- to eight-week units; helpful hints on doing legal research and holding a mock trial; discussion questions; notes on handling controversial issues, research, interviewing, and role-playing activities; additional factual information including excerpts from landmark decisions; and a seven-page annotated bibliography. Very useful in demystifying a field often frustratingly technical and remote, yet likely to be of considerable personal importance to many. The second edition adds a discussion of the past ten years, covering the ERA, cmparable worth, the alarming rise in reported incidents of domestic violence, the growing numbers of female poor, and other topics.

65. Papachristou, Judith. ***Women Together: A History in Documents of the Women's Movement in the United States.*** New York: Knopf, 1976. 270p. $15.00.

A collection of 325 documents, most a half page or less, from letters, speeches, press clippings, resolutions, and flyers. Illustrated by 135 cartoons, facsimiles, and photographs. Running commentary by the editor makes clear the historical setting. The documents are not easy reading, but with some help they could be tackled by competent 11th and 12th grade readers; slow readers can peruse the illustrations. Good for comparisons between the nineteenth and twentieth centuries.

66. Ryan, Mary P. "Reproduction in American History." ***Journal of Interdisciplinary History*** 10, no. 2 (Autumn 1979): 319–32.

In this review of three books, the author gives substantive

information about abortion and birth control from 1800 to today. Good brief introduction to major issues of this subject.

MINORITY WOMEN

General Collections

67. Blicksilver, Edith. ***The Ethnic American Woman: Problems, Protests, Lifestyles.*** Dubuque, Iowa: Kendall-Hunt, 1979. 381p. $14.95.

Over eighty contributors, in artwork, poetry, fiction, letters, short stories, reminiscences, and personal statements cover the experiences of growing up, the family, education, identity, exploitation in human relationships, work, religion and ritual, dreams and hopes, ethnic pride, and the immigrant experience. Represented are Jewish, Catholic, Mennonite, black, Hispanic-American, Asian-American, Native American, and white ethnic women. The pieces were chosen for their literary merit, and, in some cases, because they mirrored precisely "old world speech patterns." Most are contemporary, though there are a few from the nineteenth and early twentieth centuries. A wide variety of experiences and tones of voice are included, from "I am not comfortable in my yellow skin," to "Blessed the neck/of the black man made/muscular by the weight of/ the yoke made proud/bursting the lynch rope." Organization is thematic, "stressing the cycle of life," but selections are cross-indexed by genre and ethnicity. The final selection provides useful pedagogical suggestions on encouraging "ethnic girls to speak out" in writing. Listed are sixty-six thought-provoking discussion topics and classroom exercises, focusing on subject matter and style; biographical sketches of the contributors and a three-page bibliography are also provided. The readings—laconic, anguished, nostalgic, angry, funny, and fascinating—have strong personal impact. At the high school level, they could easily be woven into most required English courses, developed into a self-contained unit, or shaped into an elective course. Suitable for average readers, 9th grade and up.

68. Dodge, Diane T., Project Director. ***Shaping Teacher Expectations for Minority Girls.*** Washington, D.C.: Creative Learning, 1982. 112p. $3.00.

Designed as a "teacher training module," this booklet also provides some detailed, specific information on cultural norms, education, and job experiences for black, Puerto Rican, Mexican-American, American Indian, and Asian-American women. Strategies for meeting differing educational needs and strengths, and the formation and nature of teacher expectations, how those expectations are communicated to the students, and the effects of such expectations on student performance and feelings are dealt with. For the purposes of the high school teacher, the exercises would need to be adjusted to different levels of awareness about bias, and adapted to high school contexts, since most deal with elementary school situations. The twelve-page bibliography offers background information on minority women as well as guidelines for establishing educational equity, for creating nonsexist, nonracist educational materials, for assessing educational materials for minority and sex-role stereotyping, and for strategies to counter bias.

69. U.S. Commission on Civil Rights. ***Social Indicators of Equality for Minorities and Women.*** Washington, D.C.: U.S. Commission on Civil Rights, 1978. 136p. Free.

Twenty-four tables and twenty-four charts give information on education, unemployment rates, occupational prestige, mobility and segregation, income, homeownership, overcrowding, and relative housing costs. Some series include information since 1950, others since 1970. Most data are shown for males and females, and for American Indians, blacks, Mexican Americans, Japanese Americans, Chinese Americans, Pilipino [*sic*] Americans, Puerto Ricans, and the "majority." For ideas on using statistical data with students, see **196.**

Women of Color

70. Allman, Joanna; Scott, Patricia Bell; Hardin, Marian; and Lord, Sharon B. ***The Black Female Experience in America: A Learning/Teaching Guide.*** Newton, Mass. Education Development Center, 1979. 138p. $4.75.

"Emphasizing the growth and development of the learner," this book suggests some unusual, interesting, and successful classroom strategies, and outlines objectives and lesson plans for each of its thirteen sections. The book is organized into units titled "The Black Woman: Herstory," "Maintaining Personal Power," "Relationships, Roles and Family Life," and "Toward Healthy Development." An introduction to the relevant literature heads each section, together with a rationale for the lesson, recommended readings (some actually included, others referred to in an annotated bibliography), and suggested learning activities. The readings provided vary in difficulty; many would be accessible to high school students. Includes an eight-page annotated list of audiovisual resources.

71. Axtell, James, ed. ***The Indian Peoples of Eastern America: A Documentary History of the Sexes.*** New York: Oxford University Press, 1981. 233p. $8.95.

These sixty-seven selections are from the writings of missionaries, traders, surveyors, and diplomats. Topics covered include birth, childrearing, friendship, marriage, love charms, women's and men's work, and their roles in peace and war, religion, mythology, and death. The editor aims to "cast a wide net over the native cultures of the East" and to "cast a strong light on native people of all ages and both sexes." Unfortunately, all of the authors are white men, except for an Indian-adopted white woman and an anonymous Fox Indian woman. The introduction discusses, but minimizes, the biases this creates; the headnotes provide historical context, biographical information, and comment on the reliability of selections. This collection should be used with caution. While presentation of material on both sexes in a single volume is advantageous for use in the classroom, a number of the texts are written in a tedious style. Generally readable by competent 11th and 12th graders.

72. Elsasser, Nan; MacKenzie, Kyle; and Vigil, Yvonne Tixier y. ***Las Mujeres: Conversations from a Hispanic Community.*** Old Westbury, N.Y.: The Feminist Press, 1980. 192p. $8.95.

A collection of twenty-one women's life stories, spanning experiences from the time when New Mexico was a Spanish-speaking territory until today. The authors selected these from among ninety-three interviews seen as reflecting "common cultural concerns and customs," while also demonstrating "different personal situations, attitudes and ideas." "Pervasive major themes" are "a respect for the people, the ideas, and the customs of the past, a strong concern with women's place in the family, a desire for improved educational opportunities, a determination to work for social change." One interview is entirely in Spanish, and several others contain Spanish words and phrases, in each instance translated with respect for the original flavor. All but one have been edited to monologue form. All are vividly phrased and impressive. Illustrated with many striking photographs, both portraits and action shots. The *Teaching Guide* by Olivia Evey Chapa (39p., $4.00) gives some historical information, offers questions for discussion, and suggests activities oriented toward interviewing and oral histories. The five-page annotated bibliography includes audiovisual materials.

73. Fisher, Dexter, ed. ***The Third Woman: Minority Woman Writers of the United States.*** Boston: Houghton Mifflin, 1980. 594p. $16.50.

This anthology of nineteen American Indian, twenty-one black, nineteen Chicana, and nineteen Asian-American writers aims "to present the range, both in subject and style, of the best of the literature written by contemporary minority women in the U.S." "Multiple selections demonstrate both the linguistic and artistic versatility of individual authors," and their contribution to a developing literary tradition. Many subjects are spoken of: heritage, tradition, feminism, creativity, relationships, and identity, in genres ranging from blues poetry and personal narrative to sonnets, elegies, essays, and fiction. An introduction providing historical and cultural context precedes each section; thought-provoking discussion and writing suggestions encourage thematic, generic, and stylistic comparisons. Reading difficulty varies, but there's something here for virtually every student, 9th grade and up. Prose pieces are short enough (six to twelve pages) to provide convenient single assignments. The reading list includes anthologies and journal literature as well as primary works.

74. Garcia, Odalimira L. ***Chicana Studies Curriculum Guide: Grades 9–12.*** Austin, Tex.: Information Systems Development, 1978. 150p. $11.00.

Organized topically under such headings as the Chicana in history, society, literature, and the arts, the *Guide* outlines objectives, activities, readings, and audiovisual materials for each topic. Conventional, teacher-centered approach.

75. Green, Rayna. "Review Essay: Native American Women." ***Signs*** 6, no. 2 (Winter 1980): 248–67.

Consideration of current work is framed in the context of a chronological review of work done since the seventeenth century. It encompasses both popular and scholarly production, and the fields of anthropology, history, psychology, literature, medicine, law, and journalism in the United States and Canada. Much of this is found to have been selective, stereotyped, and damaging.

76. Kumagai, Gloria L., Project Director. ***America's Women of Color: Integrating Cultural Diversity into Non-Sex-Biased Curricula.*** Newton, Mass.: Education Development Center, 1982. 138p. $5.75.

This secondary school curriculum guide offers three lesson

plans on stereotypes and four on discrimination for grades 10 to 12, and several more for grades 7 to 9. The exercises are typically very simple: students making lists of stereotypes, students painting minority women in seldom-seen roles. Disappointing. Accompanying filmstrips ($5.25–$7.25 with *Guides*) tend to feature static groups, portraits, and a few historical photographs and charts. Filmstrip user's *Guides* reproduce the script, list questions that focus on memorization, suggest a few standard activities (scrapbooks, interviews,) and provide three pages of sketchy background information and some statistical tables. Separate, minimally annotated *Bibliography* (92p., $4.00) lists elementary, secondary, and teacher resources, including audiovisual materials. It is largely outdated and heavily technical. **70** and **297** have far more to offer.

77. Lerner, Gerda, ed. ***Black Women in White America: A Documentary History.*** New York: Random House, 1973. 672p. $8.95.

Already a classic, this important collection of over 150 documents, most of them a page or two in length, is arranged topically under headings including "Slavery," "Struggle for Education," "Woman's Lot," "Making a Living," "Race Pride," and chronologically within each section, spanning the period from 1811 to 1971. It presents the voices of black women themselves—in love, resignation, outrage, dignity, fear, rebellion, and hope. Headnotes indicate historical settings. Reading difficulty varies; for able 9th graders and up. Includes twelve pages of bibliographical notes.

78. Medicine, Bea. ***The Native American Woman: A Perspective.*** Las Cruces: New Mexico State University, 1978. 122p. $9.15. Available from Education Resource Information Center, Document Reproduction Service, 3900 Wheeler Avenue, Alexandria, Virginia 22304.

Discusses negative stereotyping of American Indian women by anthropologists and historians, and emphasizes the importance of role variations and tribal differences. The author provides a lot of detailed information on birthing, infant care, socialization, and sex roles from the "Cheyenne warrior male with a monomania for . . . military virility" for which he was both respected and pitied, to the Piegan " 'manly-hearted' women . . . [who] were accorded privileges based upon their ambition and boldness," to Hopi and Sioux treatment of rape and adultery. Much of the text is in the form of extended excerpts (twenty or so pages), in women's own words as well as from ethnographic and semi-autobiographical accounts. A number of tribes are represented, and contemporary issues (low income, sexism, the women's movement, intertribal marriage, education, identity, religion) are touched on. Judiciously chosen passages from the vivid and very graphic (some perhaps too much so for some students) personal accounts would make excellent readings for students from slow 9th graders on up.

79. Niethammer, Carolyn. ***Daughters of the Earth: The Lives and Legends of Native American Women.*** New York: Collier/Macmillan, 1977. 281p. $10.95.

Organized loosely by the life cycle from conception to burial, and topically, covering marriage, economic roles, power, war, sexuality, leisure, and religion, this book tries to "present the customs of each tribe or society as they were," before being changed by contact with Europeans. It stresses the female point of view and includes self-reports by Native American women. The simply written, flowing narrative cites songs, myths, and stories. Generally informative with interesting descriptions, though constant references to different ways of doing the same thing among different groups, and the absence of any organizing principle or theory, give a distractingly collage-like effect. Selectively assignable to competent 10th grade readers and up; note that it contains some explicit sexual descriptions and vocabulary. Illustrated with a dozen or so unusually striking black and white photographs.

80. Noble, Jeanne. ***Beautiful, Also, Are the Souls of My Black Sisters: A History of the Black Woman in America.*** Chapter 7: "Speak the Truth to the People." 62p. Englewood Cliffs, N.J.: Prentice-Hall, 1978. $14.95.

This chapter presents a concise history, hard to find elsewhere, of black women writers in America. In it, "from Phillis Wheatley to Carolyn Rodgers, one traces protest and revelation; one sees also the conflict of being spokesman for the black masses and the pull of the white world." Organized chronologically. There is some discussion of context as in accounts of, and reasons for, the Harlem Renaissance; but the focus is on a few of the works of a few major figures, summarized, discussed in detail, and quoted at some length. An introduction to the topic that could be handled by competent 11th and 12th grade readers.

Jewish Women

81. Baum, Charlotte; Hyman, Paula; and Michel, Sonya. ***The Jewish Woman in America.*** New York: New American Library, 1975. 281p. $5.95.

A narrative history that deals with Jewish women in the religious and Eastern European shtetl traditions; with the experiences of the "uptown lady" (usually of German-Jewish origin) and the "downtown woman" (usually a later migrant from Eastern Europe) in America; with education, work, and union organizing; with the changing image of the Jewish woman in literature; and with the contemporary literary, intellectual, and political protests of Jewish women against their stereotyped roles. The palatable prose is punctuated by women's voices in quotations of a sentence to half a page, from both factual and fictional accounts. Useful eighteen-page bibliography includes memoirs, autobiography, fiction, drama, and poetry, as well as historical and sociological works. Selected passages could be assigned to able 11th and 12th grade readers.

82. Elwell, Ellen Sue Levi, and Levenson, Edward R., eds. ***Jewish Women's Studies Guide.*** Fresh Meadows, N.Y.: Biblio Press, 1982. 112p. $6.95.

Fifteen syllabi outline university and adult and continuing education courses that deal with women in the Hebrew Bible; the image of Jewish women in law, literature, and liturgy; and Jewish women's roles, psychology, and writing. Included are also two essays on integrating women into historical accounts of the American Jewish experience, and a comparative study of women in the religious traditions of Judaism, Christianity, and Islam. Each syllabus gives some introductory background, a course description and outline, required readings, and suggested additional resources.

83. Heshel, Susannah, ed. ***On Being a Jewish Feminist: A Reader.*** New York: Schocken Books, 1983. 288p. $9.95.

Twenty-four articles by rabbis, professors of religious studies and history, journalists, and social workers are grouped under three headings: "Old Myths and Images," "Forging New Identities," and "Creating a Feminist Theology of Judaism," each with a brief introduction by the editor. A general introduction gives a brief history of Jewish feminism and suggests that its challenge has thrown into relief "the weakness of Jewish theological responses to modernity." Contributors consider a wide range of issues from battered Jewish wives to Israeli women, the Jewish lesbian, learning to chant the Torah, a feminine imagery of deity, and ritual. Valuable for raising questions and suggesting lines of inquiry.

84. Schneider, Susan Weidman. ***Jewish and Female: Choices and Changes in Our Lives Today.*** New York: Simon & Schuster, 1984. 448p. $19.95.

Intended as "a clearinghouse of information for . . . ways in which Jewish women are creating new realities out of their own changed consciousness," this encyclopedic resource guide presents "tales of women radical and traditional and at every stage in between." The author covers a wide range of topics, discussing women as authorities on the Jewish law, as rabbis and cantors; their adaptation of prayer garments, rewriting of liturgy, creation of rituals for the celebration of the Jewish calendar and of women's life-cycle events; how to eradicate sexism in Jewish education and scholarship; Jewish women's family and relationship issues from "the Jewish mating game" to "who marries 'out'?" and "post-Holocaust parenthood"; ways women participate in, and are supported by, the Jewish community; and Jewish women in the world of work outside the home, as "volunteers and 'professionals,'" new recruits and re-entrants, displaced homemakers, subjects of discrimination and of affirmative action.

Specific, detailed, clear, and smooth-flowing, enlivened by quotations from women of a wide variety of backgrounds, the text is authoritative and readable. Schneider clearly differentiates between information based on identified quantifiable evidence (for example, "records of night-school attendance in Pittsburgh in the 1920's"), and that from individuals (about whom enough is said to allow the reader to judge reliability, authoritativeness, and appropriateness for their own specific orientation and needs). For each topic, she presents resources, both information and action-oriented, both documentary and organizational (a bibliography on Jewish women and Jewish law is followed by a listing of institutions and individuals of use to a woman who might want to become a rabbi). A seventy-nine-page networking directory covers a wide range of topics, from alcoholism and battered women to charities, education, counseling services, the elderly, health, havurot, legal issues, lesbian and gay groups and regional contact people, immigrant services, minyanim groups and regional contact people, periodicals, singles programs, and many more. A gold mine.

Lesbian Women

85. Alyson, Sasha, ed. ***Young, Gay & Proud!*** Rev. ed. Boston: Alyson Publications, 1980. 95p. $2.95.

The authors speak directly to those high school-age students who are, or think they might be, gay. They offer advice and reassurance about coming out, dealing with friends, peers, and the fear of rejection, meeting other gays, and gay sexuality and health issues. There are some separate sections on, and for, lesbians and gay men. The tone is strained in trying to strike the right note: in attempting to be simple and colloquial, it may come across as condescending ("Psychiatrists (shrinks) . . . are special doctors who tell people the right and wrong way to behave"). There is an uneasy feeling of an "us/them" mentality, and the sections on "doing it" are very explicit in both description and terminology. "More Reading," mostly fiction, lists thirty-three titles. Suitability for use in a classroom context needs careful consideration.

86. Cruikshank, Margaret, ed. ***Lesbian Studies: Present and Future.*** Old Westbury, N.Y.: The Feminist Press, 1982. 286p. $9.95.

Aiming to "re-examine traditional ways of thinking and to replace ignorance with knowledge," the thirty contributors to this collection of essays "show by example the meaning of lesbian studies. They clarify its origins, characteristics, goals, and assumptions." Although the book "cannot claim to be comprehensive," it deals with a wide range of issues and presents various perspectives including those of Jewish women and women of color. Five essays describe "what it feels like to be a lesbian in the academic world"; nine deal with the "experience of introducing lesbian issues in the classroom"; the rest, grouped as "New Research/New Perspectives," range from a bibliography on black lesbians before 1970 to a lesbian critique of feminist literary criticism; and studies of lesbians in science, sport, history, women's studies textbooks and literature anthologies. The book includes nine sample syllabi; sixteen pages of resources, from conferences and centers to films and projects; and a thirty-five page bibliography of books and articles. Most applicable at the college level, the book could serve as a source of information and guide to the field for high school teachers also.

87. Freedman, Estelle B.; Gelpi, Barbara C.; Johnson, Susan L.; and Weston, Kathleen M., eds. ***The Lesbian Issue: Essays from* Signs.** Chicago: University of Chicago Press, 1985. 320p. $10.95.

Twelve essays by women and men, homosexuals and heterosexuals, center on "lesbian identity—its historical genesis and its relationship to both lesbian and heterosexual communities—and . . . the survival, in homophobic cultures, of women whose primary relation is to other women." Contributions include a review essay on lesbian personal narratives; reports on the Cuban lesbian and gay male experience and on discrimination against lesbians in the workforce; articles on Radclyffe Hall, Willa Cather, English boarding school friendships, sexuality, class and conflict in a lesbian workplace; a theory for lesbian readers; and book reviews.

The selections reflect, the editors feel, "the more thorough development of [lesbian] studies in literature and history," although of the forty manuscripts considered for the special issue of *Signs: Journal of Women in Culture and Society* 9, no. 4 (Summer 1984), of which this book is a reprint, "one-third were in the field of literature, another third in the social sciences, and a final third in history, anthropology, politics and theory."

88. "Special Issue—Gay and Lesbian Studies." ***Radical Teacher*** 24 (1983). Boston Women's Teachers' Group, P.O. Box 102, Kendall Square Post Office, Cambridge, Mass. 02142. $3.00.

Classroom-oriented and useful to lesbian, gay, and heterosexual teachers from the upper elementary grades to college level. Articles in this issue consider the pros and cons of "coming out" in a classroom, document sixth grade students' reactions to their teacher coming out, give a Third World feminist perspective on lesbian literature, suggest ways of dealing with heterosexism and homophobia among students and faculty, and describe the team teaching of gay and lesbian literature. Also included are book reviews and annotated bibliographies of materials for and about lesbian and gay youth that list works of fiction, autobiography, biography, history, and literature; material on minorities and Third World people; and bibliographies, directories, and teaching aids.

Disabled Women

89. Campling, Jo, ed. ***Images of Ourselves: Women with Disabilities Talking***. Boston: Routledge & Kegan Paul, 1981. 160p. $8.75.

Twenty-five English women, aged seventeen to seventy-four, with disabilities ranging from paralysis to epilepsy to deafness, talk about their lives. Their voices are down-to-earth and variously warm, wise, resigned, witty, and angry. The collection is affecting but not depressing.

90. ***Women and Disability Awareness Consciousness-Raising Packet.*** (Pilot version.) New York: Educational Equity Concepts, 1983. 41p. Write for price.

Aiming to "raise awareness about how issues of bias related to both women and disability interconnect," the packet provides background information, such as the legal definition of disability (a term preferred to "handicap"), and data on the lives of disabled women: education (44 percent of the totally disabled have eight years of elementary schooling or less), employment (about 75 percent of disabled women are unemployed, and the vocationally rehabilitated have a mean annual income of $2,744), marriage (later in life, less frequent, more divorce-prone than for nondisabled), self-image (low), and role models (lacking). The packet also suggests some "consciousness-raising questions," about a dozen of which would be applicable in a high school classroom. The readings raise some serious issues that it would be well for adolescents and young adults to confront: bearing or aborting, raising or institutionalizing a disabled child; overprotection or neglect of the disabled; rejection of those who are "different" due to the discomfort of not knowing how to behave toward them. Includes a list of resources grouped by topic. The packet would be useful background to **89.**

91. Zabolai-Csekme, Eva. ***Women and Disability.*** 2d ed. Geneva, Switzerland: United Nations, 1981. Not paginated. $6.00.

Focusing on disabled women in developing nations, "the most severely disadvantaged group in to-day's world," this kit consists of seven articles of introductory material, including data on mental illness in developing countries, training for blind rural women, love relationships among the disabled, stages of learning to live with disability, and the multiple discrimination against disabled women. This is followed by twelve pages of resources, including audiovisual materials; brief readings on disabled women and work, education, marriage, parenting, and legal and psychological considerations, with a number of excerpts from personal statements on these topics; and some simple suggestions on using these materials with groups, which could be adapted for use in high school classes. A meager offering that lacks organization and any overview of the topic—but the only thing of its kind that is available.

THE FAMILY, HOUSEWORK, AND MOTHERING

92. André, Rae. ***Homemakers: The Forgotten Workers.*** Chicago: University of Chicago Press, 1981. 320p. $8.95.

A book about the women who "wash a trillion dirty dishes a year . . . clean millions of homes [and] raise our children" but who have "earned neither salary nor security for their work," and "whose interests have often been overlooked and, worse, exploited." Important since virtually all women and an increasing number of men will be homemakers, the book describes current theories about the subject, explores how individuals think about it, outlines homemakers' problems, shows practical ways for bringing about change (from using checklists, to setting up work-sharing systems in the family, to promoting alternative lifestyles for couples and communities), and discusses organized political action by homemakers and the legislation affecting them. Trenchant thought based on sound scholarship is firmly organized and clearly expressed. Includes numerous quotations of a paragraph or so in length by and about homemakers, six interviews of two to three pages each that show "anecdotally both the delightful and the tragic sides of homemaking," a number of statistical tables, and a chapter on housework among a number of different peoples around the world. Selectively readable by competent 11th and 12th graders. Includes an eight-page bibliography.

93. Cahill, Susan, ed. ***Motherhood: A Reader for Men and Women.*** New York: Avon, 1982. 432p. $3.95.

Over fifty brief (three- to ten-page) selections by psychologists, philosophers, anthropologists, feminists, poets, and novelists, largely but not exclusively female and well known, on the celebration, opportunities, and future of motherhood, together with some cross-cultural information. Selections "reflect the sharply different and often contradictory perspectives that contemporary men and women bring to . . . motherhood." Headnotes help to give a context for individual pieces, which are based largely on feeling rather than on factual information. Useful as a source for generation of discussions; reading difficulty varies.

94. Chodorow, Nancy. ***The Reproduction of Mothering: Psychoanalysis and the Sociology of Gender.*** Berkeley: University of California Press, 1978. 263p. $7.95.

Women mother. Their doing so "is one of the few universal and enduring elements of the sexual division of labor," and has "come increasingly to define women's lives." Yet, taken for granted, this situation has rarely been analyzed. Chodorow does so.

She examines theories of mothering based on biology and on role socialization, and dismisses them in favor of psychoanalytic object-relations theory. She describes how "asymmetries in family experiences, growing out of women's mothering, affect the differential development of the male and female psyche"; discusses how the mother-infant relationship differs for girls and boys; and critiques Freudian accounts of the Oedipus complex. She finds that "a sexual division of labor in which women mother . . . [and] heterosexual marriage . . . together organize and reproduce gender as an unequal social relation." This is a scholarly book, with a fifteen-page bibliography that leans toward the technical journal literature; the conscious effort made by Chodorow to minimize psychoanalytic jargon was largely though not wholly successful. Her conclusion, that both sexes can and should parent equally, is a point also made in Dorothy Dinnerstein's *The Mermaid and the Minotaur: Sexual Arrangements and Human Malaise* (New York: Harper & Row, 1977, 288p., $4.95) which, though written by an academic, is not a scholarly book. Handling some of the same themes as Chodorow, it does so more vividly, and with an immediacy of impact that would make it good student reading, though more suitably so at the college level.

95. Cowan, Ruth Schwartz. ***More Work for Mother: The Ironies of Household Technology from the Open Hearth to the Microwave.*** New York: Basic Books, 1983. 350p. $17.95.

A history of housework ("in many ways . . . more characteristic of our society than market work," being the "occupational category that encompasses the single largest fraction of our population"), of household technology, and of the interaction between them. The author is sensitive to issues of class, to the differences between ideology and actuality, and to the relationships between household work and the market economy.

The largely chronological treatment, encompassing preindustrial conditions, early industrialization, the years between 1900–1940, and the post-war period, lends itself relatively easily to integrating the concepts and the information presented into a conventional survey course. A provocative chapter on "the roads not taken" considers alternative social and technical approaches to housework, including commercial and cooperative enterprises, domestic servants, and failed machines. The bibliographic essays accompanying each chapter suggest serendipitous further lines of thought; the text is readable and promotes reflection. The poor technical quality of the "picture essays" unfortunately impairs their impact.

96. Degler, Carl N. ***At Odds: Women and the Family in America from the Revolution to the Present.*** New York: Oxford University Press, 1980. 527p. $9.95.

A scholarly work intended for the general reader, this book tells "the story of the evolution of tension" between women and the historic family. The author argues that the existence and character of the family depend on women's subordination and discusses what this has meant "for women and the family in the past, and what it portends for . . . today and tomorrow." Based on statistical evidence and personal documents, the narrative is exhaustive and somewhat exhausting to read. It provides information on "women's activities outside the family as well as inside it, on women's participation in the paid work force, and on efforts of women to control fertility." The approach is essentially topical, with chapters arranged chronologically. Includes the experiences of poor, black, and immigrant families; and discusses theoretical questions, such as "how women's history must differ from [that] of other subordinate groups, . . . the relevance of women's sexuality to the explanation of [their] subordination," and "why the modern family and women's awakening to self emerged together at the end of the 18th century." Many fascinating quotations from primary sources are woven into the text.

97. Gutman, Herbert G. ***The Black Family in Slavery and Freedom, 1750–1925.*** New York: Random House, 1977. 664p. $6.95.

Based on quantitative data and literary records, this is a valuable source for black women's experience, showing the diversity and commonality of that experience in space and over time, and providing for it historical and theoretical contexts. This monumental revisionist study demonstrates that "large numbers of slave couples lived in long marriages, and most slaves lived in double-headed households"; and that "changes in the composition of black households over time . . . do not indicate that a 'breakdown' followed either the initial adaptation to legal freedom or early twentieth century northward migration." Includes photographic reproductions of pages from slave birth registers, drawings of family trees, and statistical tables. Excerpts, from one to several paragraphs in length that deal with a wide variety of issues in women's own proud, bitter, resigned, joyful, loving, and angry voices, could be given to high school students to analyze in class or to read as background to inquiry-oriented lessons. **77** is, however, more immediately accessible and useable for this purpose.

98. McGaw, Judith A. "Review Essay: Women and the History of American Technology." ***Signs*** 7, no. 4 (Summer 1982):798–828.

An exploration of a "rich, diverse, scattered, uneven and amorphous body of literature," the essay focuses on the technology of homemaking and of the nondomestic workplace. Briefly touched on are "technology as a tool for enhancing sex differences and reinforcing sex-role stereotypes," as in clothing and cosmetics; the differential impact on women of male-identified technologies; and technological preconditions for women's importance as consumers.

99. Scott, Donald M., and Wishy, Bernard, eds. ***America's Families: A Documentary History.*** New York: Harper & Row, 1982. 688p. $12.45.

Some 200 documents variously show "the family as idea and problem, . . . express values and ideals associated with the institution, . . . condemn the familial order and practices of others, . . . reject dominant patterns and offer alternative or counter arrangements." Letters, diaries, popular songs, laws, contracts, court records, government investigations, demographic and other statistics, advice manuals, photographs, floorplans, advertisements, and cartoons present a remarkable range of information on topics including courtship, marriage, and parenthood; black, ethnic, farm, Jewish, Catholic, Utopian, and single-headed families; abortion, adultery, birth control, divorce, and family violence; and the "politics of housework," family therapy, and families in the media. Introductions to the three broad chronological parts (spanning 1607 to the present) outline those things that had most impact on the family during each period—such as "the threat of death, the dominion of property, [and] the need for obedience and harmony" in the earliest, and the "dramatic break with biology" as well as "some husbands now tend[ing] the hearth" in the most recent period. Briefer introductions to topical sections suggest discussion questions and ways to analyze the documents as well as giving some historical and biographical information. Just reading through the introductions would suggest new perspectives on teaching familiar material in U.S. history survey courses. Reading difficulty varies; most selections are accessible to most students.

100. Shanley, Mary Lyndon. "Review Essay: The History of the Family in Modern England." ***Signs*** 4, no. 4 (Summer 1979): 740–50.

Argues for the importance of family history for the history of women, and for the need to take the economic, cultural, and intellectual context into account in studies of the family. Cites substantive information from the works discussed as well as evaluating theoretical stances.

101. Shorter, Edward. ***The Making of the Modern Family.*** New York: Basic Books, 1975. 368p. $9.95.

The author's central thesis is that "a surge of sentiment in three different areas helped to dislodge the traditional family. . . . Romantic love unseated material considerations in bringing the couple together"; "the crystallization of maternal love for infants" displaced traditional indifference; and the "Bad Old Days [when] the family's shell was pierced full of holes, permitting people from the outside to flow freely through the household" changed to a situation where "a shield of privacy was erected" and "ties binding members of the family to each other reinforced." Provocative and controversial in some of its interpretations of data, the book draws on statistical information and eyewitness accounts by clergymen, doctors, and government officials, as well as letters and poems, to create a vivid picture of the periods, events, and people discussed. Data are presented for most of Europe in the service of the argument rather than to provide a coherent picture country by country. Sharply defined ideas and Gargantuan learning are embodied in spirited, snappy prose: "The mothers would align themselves along the walls of the hall 'like a string of onions,' while the courters and the courted duelled each other on the dance floor." Includes a three-page bibliography.

102. Stone, Lawrence. "Family History in the 1980s." ***Journal of Interdisciplinary History*** 12, no. 1 (Summer 1981): 51–87.

Even for those who disagree with the author's conclusions, this is a stimulating overview of the field, including issues such as demography, household structure, economics, lineage and kin, values and emotions, and sexuality. Some of the conclusions: "Divorce . . . serves as a modern functional substitute for death"; and the "general prevalence" of infanticide, by deliberate or semideliberate neglect or direct abandonment to almost certain death, "undermines the claim that maternal love is a historical constant in all cultures, as well as a biological given."

103. Strasser, Susan. ***Never Done: A History of American Housework.*** New York: Pantheon, 1982. 365p. $11.95.

Primarily a descriptive, rather than analytical, history of the technology of housework. This work is a mine of information about the implements and techniques used by American housewives for cooking, laundering, heating, lighting, and cleaning their homes, as well as about ways in which changes in household technology affected their lives. The numerous well-chosen illustrations from contemporary sources, including photographs, advertisements, and book illustrations, are a resource in themselves.

104. Swerdlow, Amy; Bridenthal, Renate; Kelly, Joan; and Vine, Phyllis. ***Household and Kin: Families in Flux.*** Old Westbury, N.Y.: The Feminist Press, 1981. 208p. $8.95.

"Looking back to the past to trace the historical development of family forms and family ideology, reviewing and analyzing the variety of family relationships in the United States to-day, and examining Utopian alternatives to the so-called traditional family," this book shows that "the family is not only a product of the wider society, but also its producer and reproducer." The authors suggest that "changing the family can help change the society." Crammed with information and illustrated with telling examples, the plain, clear text is accessible to competent 10th grade readers and up. Ten pages of striking photographs convey some of the flavor of American families' diversity. The *Teaching Guide* by Alexandra Weinbaum and Mildred Alpern (63p., $5.00) gives detailed suggestions on how to introduce each section with sensitivity to the potentially emotion-fraught topics covered, and some unusually imaginative classroom activities, such as analyzing houseplans, acting as parents to eggs, and "envisioning the future," as well as some additional background information and a valuable five-page annotated bibliography. A new edition of *Household and Kin* is forthcoming.

WOMEN AND WORK

105. Baxandall, Rosalyn; Gordon, L.; and Reverby, S., eds. ***America's Working Women: A Documentary History, 1600 to the Present.*** New York: Random House, 1976. 408p. $8.95.

"This text defines work comprehensively: wage labor, slave labor and unpaid household labor," and focuses on working-class women. Over one hundred documents, including diaries, union records, letters, articles, songs, statistics, and photographs are grouped within chronological periods under such topics as "migrants and immigrants," "the human costs of industry," "homemaking," "war work," and "women in the Union movement." Different races, ethnic origins, and various workforce areas are represented. Each selection is preceded by a brief headnote setting it in a historical context; several pages outlining major relevant trends introduce each chronological period. Reading difficulty varies from average 9th to competent 11th and 12th grade levels.

106. Clark, Alice. ***Working Life of Women in the Seventeenth Century.*** 1919. Reprint, with introduction by Miranda Chaytor and Jane Lewis. Boston: Routledge & Kegan Paul, 1982. 368p. $9.95.

A classic account that remains unique of "the actual circumstances of women's lives" in England, whether single, married, or widowed, of upper or lower class, living in town or in the country. Court, church, and workhouse records, memoirs, letters, and account books are used to reconstruct the experiences of gentry women, who may not directly "take the pains and charge" upon themselves of "brewing, baking, kitching, milk house or malting," but, besides overseeing the work of a large household, often also engaged in trade; of "pedlars and hawkers," carrying heavy packs on their backs over long distances; of wives of day-laborers, verging on starvation whether they themselves worked for wages or not; and of the sweated laborers in the textile trades, where "we must either take this [low wage] or have no work." Clark argues that women were very productive "under conditions of Family and Domestic Industry," and that, with the change to a capitalist, wage-earning economy, the value of their contribution to the family declined, and that this had far-reaching adverse effects. The largely descriptive original account is given a theoretical framework by a new thirty-page introduction, which also refers to intervening scholarship that has questioned or modified some aspects of Clark's work. The plain, sturdy prose is flavored with many quotations from original sources, which give a strong sense of the period: "women and such impotent persons that weed corne." Some of the quotations could be selectively assigned to students of varying ability, and parts of the text to able 11th and 12th graders. Includes a twelve-page research-oriented bibliography.

107. Jensen, Joan M., ed. ***With These Hands: Women Working on the Land.*** Old Westbury, N.Y.: The Feminist Press, 1981. 320p. $9.95.

A collection of over sixty documents—letters, journals, autobiography, recorded oral accounts, excerpts from novels, myths, and poetry—and some thirty pages of historical photographs. The collection illustrates "what was most significant about the relationship of women to the land—how women felt about their work, how they learned the necessary skills to survive on the land, how their work affected those among whom they lived and labored, and the ways in which they looked at their own lives as women." In arrangement both chronological and thematic, the often striking selections portray Native American women and those moving West and remaining East in the nineteenth century; the intertwined lives of black and white women in the cotton plantation economy; the effects on women of different backgrounds of the decline in rural self-sufficiency; rural reform, and the move to the cities; and Chicana and Native American women's organizing efforts. Introductions to each section give social, economic, and historical background. The *Teaching Guide* by Joan M. Jensen (54p., $5.00) provides additional information; a standard range of projects and discussion questions; and an unusual and well-presented major activity on "Quantitative Approaches to Women's History," which demonstrates how to read the nineteenth-century manuscript census, gives questions to help interpret the data, and includes a set of four statistical tables relevant to farm women. The five-page annotated bibliography also lists records and films.

108. Kessler-Harris, Alice. ***Out to Work: A History of Wage-Earning Women in the United States.*** New York: Oxford University Press, 1982. 400p. $8.95.

The central concern throughout this book is the interplay between the ideology that woman's place is in the home, and the economic as well as psychological realities that have contributed to her increasing work outside the home. The topic of wage work by women is exhaustively covered, from a Boston "Manufactory" of 1750, opened as an alternative to the workhouse for "women and children who are now in great measure idle"; to the 10 percent who took jobs outside their homes in 1840, though a great many more took work into the home; to the expansion of labor force participation by women in the nineteenth century (seen as an "unfortunate necessity," interfering with their more desirable work at home and condoned by employers who hired women because they were supposed to be docile, expect no advancement, and lack union consciousness); to direct competition with men for jobs in the early twentieth century; to the contemporary situation, where "home and work roles, seemingly complementary in the preindustrial period and tightly regulated thereafter, [have] . . . burst their constraints." Authoritative but not stodgy.

109. Kessler-Harris, Alice. ***Women Have Always Worked: An Historical Overview.*** Old Westbury, N.Y.: The Feminist Press, 1980. 208p. $9.95.

The central theme here is the relationship between women's work in and out of the home. After an introductory chronological survey, information is presented by topic: work in the home, work for wages, social work, and contemporary changes. Within each section, the treatment is roughly chronological once again. Using both anecdotal and statistical modes, and sensitive to differences of race, class, ethnic origin, geography, and the urban/rural split, the text is liberally laced with quotations from primary sources. Illustrated with striking and illuminating photographs, this volume is useful both in itself and as supplementary reading in courses using traditional texts. For competent 10th grade readers and up. The *Teaching Guide* by Alexandra Weinbaum (67p., $5.00) provides classroom strategies, additional information, thought-provoking discussion questions and activities, and a nine-page annotated bibliography that includes audiovisual materials.

110. Ruddick, Sara, and Daniels, Pamela, eds. ***Working It Out: 23 Women Writers, Artists, Scientists, and Scholars Talk about Their Lives and Work.*** New York: Pantheon, 1978. 349p. $7.95.

"What is the place of chosen work in women's lives?" The editors' respondents answer in very personal terms, reflecting on their "efforts to define and pursue 'work of their own' and to overcome the inner and outer obstacles to the legitimacy of such work." Includes accounts by Alice Walker, May Stevens, Naomi Weisstein, and Tillie Olsen, as well as less well-known figures; and brief biographical sketches of the contributors. Illustrated with portraits and with photographs of works by those in the visual arts. The selections are eminently readable.

111. Tilly, Louise A., and Scott, Joan W. ***Women, Work, and Family.*** New York: Holt, Rinehart and Winston, 1978. 274p. $17.95.

A history of the economic, demographic, and familial influences on women's work, this book asks: How many, and who, were the women who worked, and why did they do so? It compares urban and rural working women, and conditions in France and England, since about 1700, and shows that there are clear continuities in the work of women before, during, and after industrialization. Scholarly but reasonably readable, the text is liberally studded with quotations of a sentence to a paragraph in length from original sources, and with statistical tables and graphs. Much of the nine-page bibliography is technical and specialized.

112. U.S. Department of Labor, Bureau of Labor Statistics. ***Perspectives on Working Women: A Data Book.*** Washington, D.C.: Bureau of Labor Statistics, 1980. Available from the U.S. Government Printing Office. 105p. $5.50.

One hundred tables provide information on women's labor force participation: unemployment rates, occupational distribution, part-time work, "moonlighting," earnings and hours worked; marital and family status; and school enrollment. Nineteen tables give information by race and Hispanic origin. Many refer both to women and men; some include figures from the 1950s, others cover shorter time series. For suggestions about ways to use statistics in the classroom, see **196.**

113. U.S. Department of Labor, Bureau of Labor Statistics. ***Women at Work: A Chartbook.*** Washington, D.C.: Bureau of Labor Statistics, Bulletin 2168, April 1983. Available from the U.S. Government Printing Office. 29p. $4.00.

Fifteen large-scale charts show changes in women's labor force participation and in their full-time housekeeping role, including information on full- and part-time work, occupational distribution, unemployment, earnings, employment of married women and mothers, and female-headed families.

114. Walshok, Mary L. ***Blue Collar Women: Pioneers on the Male Frontier.*** Garden City, N.Y.: Anchor/Doubleday, 1981. 336p. $7.95.

Based on and quoting extensively from interviews with one hundred California women welders, carpenters, mechanics, and machinists, this book would be particularly useful in demonstrating the diversity of women's lives and experiences, while providing students with possible role models to follow. It shows that work is central to these women's identities, that "they are highly motivated," that they "want autonomy and control of the work process," and that they see their jobs as satisfying—in spite of "often harrowing" initial experiences. The interview excerpts, from which teachers would need to choose the most relevant passages for their purposes, are readable by average 9th graders.

GENDER ROLES

115. David, Deborah S., and Brannon, Robert, eds. ***The Forty-Nine Percent Majority: The Male Sex Role.*** Reading, Mass.: Addison-Wesley, 1976. 352p. $12.95.

An interdisciplinary anthology of thirty-seven selections ranging from personal experience to scholarly analysis, research reports, journalistic reportage, and excerpts from interviews and case studies, this book deals with psychological, sociological, legal, and political aspects of the male role. A forty-one-page introductory essay supplies a context and touches on the main issues. The selections include pieces on men as parents; homophobia; work in the factory, office, and academe; violence in war, literature, and sports; socialization; and attempts at changing the role of the male. Sensitive to issues of class and sexual orientation, though less so to race. Most of the selections are very readable and could be assigned to students in the upper grades. Some four-letter words.

116. Dubbert, Joe L. ***A Man's Place: Masculinity in Transition.*** Englewood Cliffs, N.J.: Prentice-Hall, 1979. 323p. $5.95.

This general narrative survey of the American middle- and upper middle-class masculine image is based largely on secondary sources and a sampling of autobiographies. The author argues that "the very terms of the dream—the vigor of the masculine paradigm embracing intense individualism, free enterprise, the self-made man ideal, the moral athlete . . . contained within it certain doubts and frustrations . . . [that] often cut off [men] from one another, from families, and even from culture and social change." He examines the part played in the development of the image by the idea and reality of "the frontier," the Depression, sports, women, and feminism; as well as the influence of role models, from a "he-man Christ" to Daniel Boone, Theodore Roosevelt, and Jack Armstrong. A wider range of this subject is covered by **126** (Western civilization, rather than North American, and considers the working class as well as the middle class); best choice on this subject is still **117.**

117. Filene, Peter Gabriel. ***Him/Her/Self: Sex Roles in Modern America.*** New York: New American Library, 1975. 326p. $3.50.

"How have middle-class men and women defined themselves during the eighty-five years from the late Victorian era to the present? Why have these definitions changed? What psychological and intellectual dilemmas have people undergone, and perhaps resolved, as they tried to find satisfactory roles?" In answering these questions, the author explores themes of "feminism, employment, child-rearing, sexuality, among others," crossing "the boundaries of political, economic, intellectual, demographic and other kinds of history." Written with style, intelligence, and sensitivity, and packed with fascinating information, it is readable if slightly overwhelming. The bibliographic essay is still useful, especially for personal and fictional histories. Portions could be read by able 11th and 12th graders.

118. Harrison, James B. "Review Essay: Men's Roles and Men's Lives." ***Signs*** 4, no. 2 (Winter 1978): 324–36.

Discusses the traditional paradigm for social science research on gender differences, and the changes taking place in response to feminist analyses. According to the "emerging perspective," the cultural "construct *m/f* [masculine/feminine] becomes unnecessary for psychological research and theory."

119. Miller, Barbara; Johnson, Jacquelyn; and Foster, Joanne S. ***A Comparative View of the Roles of Women and Men.*** Rev. ed. Denver: Center for Teaching International Relations, 1976. 104p. $14.95.

The title is misleading. Only a few of the thirty-plus largely self-contained "activities," geared to grade levels 6 through 12, deal significantly with women from other cultures, nor is the focus a comparison of male and female roles. There are no suggestions for background reading, no context, and no theoretical background. Suggested activities, typically planned to take up one to four class periods, are simplistic to the point of being occasionally misleading, and consist of discussion, letters to media, dioramas, mobiles, and interviewing. Disappointing and expensive.

120. Miller, Patricia Y., and Fowlkes, Martha R. "Review Essay: Social and Behavioral Constructions of Female Sexuality." ***Signs*** 5, no. 4 (Summer 1980): 783–800.

A critique of significant work in the field, revealing that "there has yet to emerge anything that resembles a dominant paradigm organizing the study and interpretation of female sexuality."

121. Pleck, Joseph H. ***The Myth of Masculinity.*** Cambridge: MIT Press, 1981. 240p. $7.95.

"This book critically analyzes the . . . set of ideas about sex roles, especially the male role, that has dominated the academic social sciences since the 1930's and . . . has shaped our culture's view of the male role." The author identifies the characteristics of the "male sex role identity paradigm" underlying traditional social science and cultural studies. Such studies hold that "sex roles develop from within, rather than being arbitrarily imposed from without," and, ideally, derive from the relationship with the same-sex parent; that, for their own good, individuals must develop the appropriate roles; and that the problem "is only that so many people fail to fit them, not the nature of the roles." He also outlines an alternative, the "sex role strain paradigm," being developed by "social scientists influenced by feminist analysis." Unlike the traditional paradigm, which assumes "an *innate psychological need* for sex-typed traits," central arguments of the new paradigm concern "the implications of sex-typed traits for *social approval* and *situational adaptation*." This is a dense, analytical, and, to an extent, technical work; it is also challenging, thought-provoking, informative, and readable by the persevering nonspecialist. Includes a twenty-six-page bibliography.

122. Richmond-Abbott, Marie. ***Masculine and Feminine: Sex Roles over the Life Cycle.*** Reading, Mass.: Addison-Wesley, 1983. 434p. $14.95.

The author tries "to trace the process and the reasons why we are socialized into traditional roles so that we can see the sources of our own oppression," whether we are male or female. In clear, smooth prose aimed at a college student audience, she discusses the biological, environmental, ideological, and economic roots of women's lower social status; socialization by parents, toys, the media, and schools; adolescence, including the masculine and feminine "worlds" in high school, the experience of black high school girls, dating, and sexuality; the "ideal family" (for both adult females and males), family variants (childless, dual-career, single-parent, remarried, blue-collar, black, violent), and family alternatives (being single); men and women at work and in politics; and possibilities for the future. Throughout, the experiences of different races and classes are discussed in significant detail. Each of the eleven chapters is followed by essay/discussion questions and suggestions for thought-provoking and interesting exercises, some of which could be used with high school students. While there is some overlap in subject matter with **304** and **307,** this book is simpler and more directly relevant to high school needs than those are, though it is less thorough.

123. Rubin, Michael. ***Men without Masks: Writings from the Journals of Modern Men.*** Reading, Mass.: Addison-Wesley, 1980. 228p. $6.95.

Excerpts from the journals of thirty twentieth-century men, some famous and some unknown, who "used their hearts as much as their heads as they wrote about their daily lives." The author hopes that this book "will make more women as well as men aware of the particular difficulties that we men face." The selections focus on the themes of Sons; Idealists; Lovers, Husbands and Fathers; Working Men; Explorers; and Aging and Dying Men. Brief headnotes set the context for each excerpt. A good companion volume to **169.**

124. Sadker, David. ***Being a Man: A Unit of Instructional Activities on Male Role Stereotyping.*** Washington, D.C.: U.S. Government Printing Office, 1977. 64p. $5.00.

Starting with Lesson One: "Stifle It," this booklet gives concise basic background information for teachers on the nature and costs of the masculine mystique. Eight units outline objectives, define concepts, and provide detailed lesson plans with discussion questions and reproducible materials for student use. Intelligent, sensitive, pithy, and thought-provoking, it was designed for junior high school students but would be useable with 9th and 10th graders.

125. Sargent, Alice G. ***Beyond Sex Roles.*** New York: West Publishing, 1977. 489p. $18.95.

The author is concerned with "the role liberation of women and men so that each of us has the potential to develop a role-free human identity which encompasses both male and female characteristics—androgyny." She writes about the skills necessary for this development: "autonomy, intimacy and interdependence"; and the restructuring of institutions that currently "maintain the status quo." About one-third of this "didactic and experiential" workbook consists of fifty-eight exercises that can be used by individuals or in groups, each consisting of a goal, directions, and explanation. The exercises range from simple sentence completion in "The Ethnic Me," to role-playing, group dynamics, and simulation. Most are selectively suitable for classroom use with 9th grade students and up. Twenty-five informative and provocative essays by well-known psychologists, sociologists, and linguists, including "The Competitive Male as Loser," "Womanspeak and Manspeak," "Sisterhood is Complicated," "The Changing Place of Work for Women and Men," "Racism, Sexism and Class Elitism," and "Teachers as Mediators of Sex Role Standards," complete the volume.

126. Stearns, Peter N. ***Be a Man! Males in Modern Society.*** New York: Holmes & Meier, 1979. 230p. $12.75.

In part a straight social history based largely but not exclusively on secondary sources, and focusing on industrialization as pivotal in the changes in men's image and role; and in part a more personal interpretation of and commentary on contemporary social science, feminist, and reform stances on gender roles. The former is more successful. The narrative deals with Western society and its traditional definitions of manhood in the seventeenth and eighteenth centuries, with the "crisis of masculinity" that began with the modernization process" and "questioned conventional notions of masculinity . . . from physical strength to property ownership," with the development of working- and of middle-class versions of manhood, and with the contemporary search for greater flexibility in male roles. Aimed at a general rather than a narrowly scholarly audience. Valuable for its treatment of working-class men, though **117** is still the better choice.

127. Tavris, Carol, and Wade, Carole. ***The Longest War: Sex Differences in Perspective.*** 2d ed. New York: Harcourt Brace Jovanovich, 1984. 416p. $14.95.

Lively, readable, and scholarly, this book is a mine of information without being stodgy on biological, psychological, educational, sociological, and historical aspects of the topic. Discusses the real and imagined differences between women and men in abilities and personality; the Victorian legacy of sexuality, and its scientific study; genes, hormones, and instincts; the Freudian psychoanalytical perspective and its critique; socialization theories and their practice by parents, teachers, and media; work and marriage; anthropological theories about reasons for "male dominance and variations in female status across cultures and throughout history"; and case studies of egalitarian experiments in the U.S.S.R., China, Sweden, and Israel. An *Instructor's Manual* is available. Selected passages could be assigned to competent 11th and 12th grade readers.

ART

PERFORMING ARTS

128. Ammer, Christine. ***Unsung: A History of Women in American Music.*** Westport, Conn.: Greenwood Press, 1980. 317p. $7.95.

Focusing "especially on the lives and work of outstanding individuals," this book tells the story of instrumentalists, conductors, composers, and teachers during the past two centuries. Artists discussed include Sophie Hewitt, whose piano playing was praised as "plain sensible and that of a Gentlewoman" in 1822, Amy Beach, whose advice to young composers in 1915 was that they should "feel deeply," and Victoria Bond, "the first woman admitted to Juilliard as a doctoral candidate in conducting," who received her degree in 1977. Written in plain prose with some quotations from original sources, the book lacks focus and offers no historical, psychological or feminist analysis. It is, however, reasonably readable, though the style smacks of that in encyclopedia articles. There is nothing better available in this subject area. Includes a ten-page bibliography.

129. Chinoy, Helen Krich, and Jenkins, Linda Walsh, eds. ***Women in American Theatre: Careers, Images, Movements.*** New York: Crown, 1981. 384p. $4.98.

Fifty essays and interviews explore the less-well known rather than rehashing the lives of major figures. Organized into sections on female rites (in beauty pageants, in political parties, by Native American women); actresses; playwrights (from Mercy Otis Warren, "satirist of the Revolution," to the "autonomous women" and choral plays of the 1970s); careers (a "mélange of autobiographies, memoirs, interviews and notes" covering "producers, directors, designers, casting specialists and teachers"); images (women in melodrama, in Pulitzer Prize plays, black women in plays by black writers); and feminist theater. Selections range from scholarly to chatty, and vary in quality and importance. Less directly useful in a classroom setting than in sparking insights into or broadening the reader's outlook on the American theater scene in general. Includes a twenty-seven-page listing of sources and resources, and thirty-two pages of illustrations.

130. Henderson, Kathy, with Armstrong, Frankie, and Kerr, Sandra. ***My Song Is My Own: One Hundred Women's Songs.*** London: Pluto Press, 1981. Available from Legacy Books. 192p. $7.95.

A collection intended for use as a songbook, this book presents British women's songs from the fifteenth century to the present as single line music and guitar chords. Traditional and broadside ballads, industrial, strike, music hall, variety, folk, and children's songs, and those from the contemporary women's movement and feminist theater are included. The collection "reflects the experience of ordinary women, throws light on their lives and feelings, and links up the largely invisible tradition of women's resistance." Songs are grouped thematically under headings of Love (some refer to sexual behavior, though not in a verbally explicit way), Marriage, Motherhood, and Work, with an introduction to each section and brief notes, including the composition date, for most songs. A fascinating anthology.

131. Malpede, Karen, ed. ***Women in Theater: Compassion and Hope.*** New York: Drama Book Publishers, 1983. 304p. $19.95.

A fuzzily conceived anthology of writings by actresses, critics, dancers, playwrights, producers, directors, and writers of feminist plays. Headnotes of a couple of pages give some information about the lives and ideas of the authors. The twenty or so selections vary from a historical and critical account of the tenth-century nun and playwright Hroswitha to interviews, letters, diaries, lectures, and program notes with, by, and about Kemble, Terry, Le Gallienne, Duncan, Dunham, Graham, Hansberry, Stein, Goldman, and others. A readable variety of offerings with a frustrating lack of focus.

132. Neuls-Bates, Carol, ed. ***Women in Music: An Anthology of Source Readings from the Middle Ages to the Present.*** New York: Harper & Row, 1982. 384p. $17.79.

Aims to present "vivid, contemporary accounts of women musicians both notable and lesser-known, including composers, performers, patrons and educators, most often told in the words of the women themselves." Included are letters, diaries, autobiographies, interviews, newspaper accounts, and reviews of performances, introduced by headnotes that provide a context. Describes how some women have "been able to obtain the encouragement, training, opportunities necessary for a professional career"; and illustrates musicians' lives by examples of the advice given to women about their proper role in music. Liveliness of selections varies; most are accessible to competent readers.

133. Noble, Jeanne. ***Beautiful, Also, Are the Souls of My Black Sisters: A History of the Black Woman in America.*** Chapter 8: "When Malindy Sings." 78p. Englewood Cliffs, N.J.: Prentice Hall, 1978. $14.95.

This survey, hard to find anywhere else, traces black women's music from "The African Past" through "The Blues" and "Broadway" to "Soul Singers" and "The Classical Malindys." Largely an account of individuals, with ample quotations from a sentence to a paragraph or two from critical reviews, poems, songs, and the women's own words, the author has paid little attention to historical or social context. Readable by competent 11th and 12th graders.

134. Wood, Elizabeth. "Review Essay: Women in Music." ***Signs*** 6, no. 2 (Winter 1980): 283–97.

An examination of the last five years' research, which shows concentration on source documentation to the neglect of theory, and on rewriting women into the conventional historical narrative rather than creating feminist analysis.

VISUAL ARTS

135. Allen, Virginia. "The Naked Lady: A Look at Venus in the Renaissance." ***Feminist Art Journal*** (Spring 1977): 27–29, 50.

Brief but useful account of changes in women's status at the time of the Renaissance. Considers education, law, economics, ideology, and symbolic expression in painting.

136. Cole, Doris. ***From Tipi to Skyscraper: A History of Women in Architecture.*** Cambridge: MIT Press, 1978. 136p. $5.95.

Documenting the contributions of American women architects through the years, and written in straightforward prose, this book deals with "Pioneers and Indians," the "Domestic Domain" in early America, "Social Transitions" from the domestic circle to the civic arena, the education of women as architects, and the role of female architects in contemporary practice. The forty-five striking illustrations, from archival nineteenth-century photographs to houseplans, interiors, and female architects at work are a resource in themselves. Excellent introduction to a barely touched-on field; readable by competent 10th graders and up.

137. Fine, Elsa Honig. ***Women and Art: A History of Women Painters and Sculptors from the Renaissance to the 20th Century.*** Montclair, N.J.: Abner Schram, 1978. 240p. $38.50.

A look at ninety-three painters and sculptors, none of them women of color, "who have achieved wide recognition." The book is organized by country and genre, but is roughly chronological in sequence ("The French Academic Tradition," "The English School: Portraiture"). Each chapter looks first at the role and status of women in a country and period, followed by an analysis of the lives and works of women artists and how they coped with their various responsibilities. The historical information on the Renaissance does not reflect the new scholarship on women. Complements rather than duplicates **144,** while covering much the same ground with a less feminist stance, a duller style, more detail on fewer people, and better reproductions (some in color).

138. Greer, Germaine. ***The Obstacle Race: The Fortunes of Women Painters and Their Work.*** New York: Farrar Straus Giroux, 1979. 373p. $12.95.

Excluding living painters, the author "marshal[s] a whole crowd of women, some of whom have left a single good work, some no work at all and more a patchy, poorly preserved cluster of forgotten effort," instead of presenting only the well known. She tells about her subjects' lives and work, using their own words or those of contemporaries; offers a technical discussion and critical evaluation of individual paintings ("she continues to use the warm, reverberant jewel colors of a more formalistic epoch"); and makes psychological observations ("for hundreds of women artists, the abandonment of a domestic role was expiated by the daily depiction of idyllic domestic scenes"). Lapses into sexist language suggest that none of us is immune to conditioning; and patches of a dozen or so names crowding on each other with little or no discussion are an occasional minor irritation. The style is gutsy and unpretentious; the scholarship has been criticised. When speculative, it is identifiably so. Includes 326 adequate to very good black and white reproductions, and 32 excellent color reproductions. A good source for teacher background.

139. Harris, Anne Sutherland, and Nochlin, Linda. ***Women Artists: 1550–1950.*** Los Angeles County Museum of Art/New York: Knopf, 1977. 367p. $19.95.

Based on the first international exhibition of art by women, 204 high-quality plates, 32 in color, illustrate the works of 84 artists in painting, drawing, and graphic arts. Two introductory essays provide historical background, including information on the status and education of women in general and of artists as a group, and institutional aspects of artists' careers such as patronage, membership in academies, and professional training. Individual commentaries include, besides biographies, a bluntly critical discussion of works. Scholarly but not stodgy; useful for teacher background and possible student reference. Little overlap with **144** in the works illustrated.

140. Hedges, Elaine, and Wendt, Ingrid. ***In Her Own Image: Women Working in the Arts.*** Old Westbury, N.Y.: The Feminist Press, 1980. 308p. $9.95.

Poetry, fiction, autobiography, essays, journal excerpts, letter writing, painting, graphics, sculpture, photography, ceramics, needlework, music, and dance are represented here, some by women of color. These examples are intended to "illustrate the nature, the breadth and the diversity of women's work in the arts . . . in a variety of western societies and historical periods," and to relate "women's art [to] the condition of women's lives." Headnotes provide biographical data and context. The organization is thematic rather than chronological, but the four sections, each with an introduction of ten pages or so, suggest stages in the development of women, both as a group and as individuals, as they become professional artists—from involvement with household art, through obstacles and challenges, to self-definition, and working for social change. Includes fifty-seven black and white illustrations. Recommended for competent 10th grade readers and up. The *Teaching Guide* by Ingrid Wendt (53p., $5.00) provides thought-provoking discussion questions and an eleven-page annotated bibliography.

141. Loeb, Judy, ed. ***Feminist Collage: Educating Women in the Visual Arts.*** New York: Teachers College Press, 1979. 317p. $14.95.

Twenty-eight articles by scholars, critics, artists, and teachers examine "three major changes in the art world . . . initiated by feminists" in the 1970s: reappraisals of art and art history, reexaminations of artists and society, and restructurings of art education. Titles include "Past and Present Inequities in Art Education,"

"Women of Surrealism," "The Significance of What Boys and Girls Choose to Draw," "The Male Artist as a Stereotypical Female," and "Architecture: Towards a Feminist Critique." Interesting but not high-priority background reading for teachers.

142. Munro, Eleanor. ***Originals: American Women Artists.*** New York: Simon & Schuster, 1982. 528p. $14.95.

Studies of forty-four contemporary women, spanning three generations, which "fall between and include elements of biography and autobiography, interview, profile and impression." The author offers some generalizations about her subjects: the freshness and "special, vivid interest" to the artists of their childhood memories; that they "worked with the content of their lives, and knew it"; that they were inhibited in their artistic development by "the taboo against women in male bonding places"; and that, having come from educated middle-class or art-appreciating immigrant families (including the four black artists), "the process of self-acceptance [was made] easier." An introductory chapter sets "the new woman artist" into historical context; the rest of the book is a combination of direct quotations from interviews and the author's insightful and sometimes baroque commentary (e.g., "for Krasner, in this instance, collage was both sword and ploughshare, a handle to savage, and salvage, the early works by cutting them into lots and rooting them into new compositions"). Numerous well-reproduced illustrations and some striking color plates show works of art as well as artists, some of them at work. Each section could be assigned to an individual student to report on in class; recommended for competent 11th and 12th grade readers.

143. Parker, Rozsika, and Pollock, Griselda. ***Old Mistresses: Women, Art, and Ideology.*** New York: Pantheon, 1982. 184p. $10.95.

In loosely chronological order, the authors discuss the lives, careers, and works (concentrating on imagery rather than technique) of women in the visual arts, in the context of both their historical setting and in comparison with male artists. Also discussed are the hierarchy of art forms that differentiates the public and performing fine arts from the domestic arts or crafts along both class and sex lines, changes in the ideology and definition of the artist, and the feminine stereotype in art. Intriguing to those with an interest in the topic, it is the most feminist and theoretical of the books on art listed. A good source for teacher education; readable by nonspecialists. The ninety-seven black and white illustrations often compare male and female treatment of the same subject.

144. Petersen, Karen, and Wilson, J. J. ***Women Artists: Recognition and Reappraisal from the Early Middle Ages to the Twentieth Century.*** New York: Harper & Row, 1976. 212p. $9.13.

"Intended as a general historical overview of women artists working in the Western tradition," with an appendix on China, this book concentrates on the lives and self-concepts of 150 artists, and on their relationships to their historical settings, their families, and other artists of their time, rather than on their art. The 330 black and white illustrations (on the whole well reproduced, though in some the detail is lost) "must speak for themselves." Includes sculptors as well as painters. The lively, sometimes chatty text includes copious quotations mostly from writings by, and some about, the artists. Competent 11th and 12th graders could read it.

145. Rubinstein, Charlotte Streifer. ***American Women Artists: From Early Indian Times to the Present.*** New York: Avon, 1982. 576p. $12.95.

Organized by historical periods and genres in painting and sculpture, "the purpose of this book is not merely to add women to existing art histories, but also to show the relation between women's art and their social and cultural circumstances." Heading each chapter is an outline of the historical setting, including women's position, and a discussion, mercifully free of jargon, of the prevailing art styles. Entries from a paragraph to several pages in length on individual artists, grouped by style, follow. Each combines biographical details with descriptions and evaluations of works, interspersed with brief exerpts from statements by the artists and their critics. Includes separate sections on Native American, Chicana, and Latina artists, and on Folk Art; women of color are also represented in the various periods covered. Illustrated with 235 crisp black and white and 49 color illustrations. Competent 11th and 12th graders could read selections.

146. Russell, H. Diane. "Review Essay: Art History." ***Signs*** 5, no. 3 (Spring 1980): 468–81.

Deals with scholarship concerned with recovery of information about the lives and works of hitherto neglected women artists, with questions of a characteristically female imagery, and with the imagery of women in the works of male artists.

147. Torre, Susana, ed. ***Women in American Architecture: A Historic and Contemporary Perspective.*** New York: Watson-Guptill, 1977. 224p. $26.50.

The result of an exhibition, this book documents a story "tied to historical and social trends" and not "dominated by key figures"; and reveals "the range and quality of women's work as architects, planners and designers." It also tells about art and technology, vernacular as well as monumental architecture, the organization of space, and the needs of a changing society; about what helped and hindered women architects, what training they had access to, when, how, and what they were commissioned to design, what efforts they made on their own behalf, and "what are the interrelationships of woman as consumer, producer, critic and creator of space." Thirteen articles by different contributors explore model domestic space and challenges to it, women in the profession in five chronological periods, current projects, and women's spatial symbolism. Beautifully produced, the book has about as many pages of illustrations as text, including archival photographs, pictures of interiors and facades, urban plans, artwork, portraits, and houseplans, which could be used immediately and directly in the classroom (for suggestions on how, see **183** and **104**). Brimful of information and ideas couched in palatable prose.

ENGLISH

LANGUAGE AND COMMUNICATION

148. Goffman, Erving. ***Gender Advertisements.*** New York: Harper & Row, 1979. 84p. $8.95.

Over five hundred "unrandomly collected" advertisements and news photographs that show women and men are grouped here into sets with themes ("Relative Size," "The Feminine Touch," "The Family," "The Ritualization of Subordination," and "Licensed Withdrawal") that bear "on gender, especially female gender, and [are] arranged with malice within each set to the same end." Brief commentary to each set draws attention to subtle details of hands, eyes, and stance, which show "social weight," expressed in such things as relative size; in women's hands pictured as cradling, caressing, or barely touching, rather than grasping, manipulating, or holding; and in women receiving rather than giving instruction or help. Useful for suggestions on ways to analyze advertisements, an exercise often assigned to students, and for pointing out some of the problems usually encountered in such analysis. Comparisons with student-collected advertisements could be made: Are the same themes still handled in the same way? The thirty-page introductory text is dense and difficult, but concise, challenging, and rewarding. It "speculates richly on what [advertisements showing women and men] tell us about ourselves [and] what the interplay is between fashioned image and so-called natural behavior." Text for teachers only; black and white pictures suitable for use with all students.

149. Kramer, Cheris; Thorne, Barrie; and Henley, Nancy. "Review Essay: Perspectives on Language and Communication." ***Signs*** 3, no. 3 (Spring 1978): 638–51.

Discusses scholarship on the differences between women and men in speech and nonverbal communication, the social context of language use and its effects, sexism in language, and prospects for change.

150. Miller, Casey, and Swift, Kate. ***Words and Women.*** Garden City, N.Y.: Doubleday, 1977. 177p. $3.95.

Clear, good-humored, balanced summary of the issues in sexist language. Some of the material would be easily adaptable for use in the classroom by the teacher; could be assigned as reading to interested and competent 11th and 12th graders. Authoritative but not intimidating.

151. Nilsen, Alleen Pace. ***Changing Words in a Changing World: Pop! Goes the Language.*** Newton, Mass.: Education Development Center, 1979. 73p. $2.00. *Teacher's Guide.* 32p. $1.75.

Focusing on the "differences between language by and about males and females," this booklet for precollege students suggests the impact of this dimension of language on the self-images and roles of women and men. The text introduces four linguistic principles that demonstrate the relationship between language and society, and provides opportunities for students to analyze metaphors, names, captions to advertisements, and occupational terms to see what these reveal about cultural values and expectations. Each of the four sections has imaginative suggestions for Field Work (it would be worth analyzing the differences in connotation between this term and Activity, the more usual word in textbooks), Analysis, Discussion, and Composition. The book would work well as a unit in most high school English courses.

152. Nilsen, Alleen Pace; Bosmajian, Haig; Gershuny, H. Lee; and Stanley, Julia P. ***Sexism and Language.*** Urbana, Ill.: National Council of Teachers of English, 1977. 203p. $9 non-members, $6.50 members.

Eight articles by four authors address "linguistic sexism as a social issue," and examine sexist language in vocabulary, literature, dictionaries and texts, children's books and elementary teaching materials, and in the languages of legislatures, the courts, and in marriage. The material is stimulating, good-humored, clearly argued, soundly documented, well balanced, and mercifully clear of academic jargon. Can be used as a springboard to ideas for classroom exercises. The brief appendix of "Guidelines for Nonsexist Use of Language" gives easy-to-follow steps for ridding language of sexism in areas within everyone's control: everyday speech, correspondence, reports, and proposals.

153. Thorne, Barrie; Kramer, Cheris; and Henley, Nancy, eds. ***Language, Gender and Society.*** Rowley, Mass.: Newbury House Pubs., 1983. 342p.

A concise introduction provides an overview of the issues and research findings in the field. Nine essays, by psychologists, linguists, sociologists, and English-language scholars, focus on sex bias in everyday language and its effects on cognition, attitudes, and behavior; the importance of social context in language use; the implications of conversational interaction for social power; and genre and style in women's writing. Includes a 178-page annotated bibliography of "Sex Similarities and Differences in Language, Speech and Nonverbal Communication." Scholarly but readable by the nonspecialist.

154. Tuchman, Gaye; Daniels, Arlene Kaplan; and Benét, James, eds. ***Hearth and Home: Images of Women in the Mass Media.*** New York: Oxford University Press, 1978. 333p. $11.95.

Fourteen articles, based on original research by recognized scholars in psychology, sociology, and communications, examine television, women's magazines, and women's pages of the newspapers for their portrayal of, and possible impact on, women. Central to the discussions are the ideas that "the mass media reflect dominant social values," and that, in the media surveyed, women "are subject to symbolic annihilation" by condemnation, trivialization, and absence. The researchers have found that "the media encourage their audiences to engage in . . . stereotyping," and "lead girls, in particular, to believe that their social horizons and alternatives are more limited than is actually the case." Some recommendations about remedying this situation are made. Combines solid, factual information with challenging ideas; could serve as background to students' own research. Designing projects for students of all ages based on the information given would be relatively easy. Selectively readable by interested and competent 11th and 12th graders.

155. U.S. Commission on Civil Rights. ***Window Dressing on the Set: An Update.*** Washington, D.C.: U.S. Commission on Civil Rights, 1979. 97p. Free.

This volume augments, with information on the mid-1970s, the 1977 volume (also available free) that studies the 1950s to the 1970s. Information on how minorities and women have been portrayed on television in drama, situation comedies, newsstories, and on the efforts and results of equal employment opportunity policies in the field of television is given. The 1977 volume allows some comparisons to be made by decade and between different minority groups. Both volumes provide data on race, sex, occupation, victimization ratios, and relative proportions of heroes and villains of the characters shown on television. Both also deal with the employment of minorities and women in local and network television, and with the effects of television on children. Almost exclusively factual; the 1977 volume contains more than fifty tables, the 1979 volume more than thirty.

LITERATURE

156. Bankier, Joanna; Cosman, Carol; Earnshaw, Doris; Keefe, Joan; Lashgari, Deirdre; and Weaver, Kathleen, eds. ***The Other Voice: Twentieth-Century Women's Poetry in Translation***. New York: W. W. Norton, 1976. 218p. $5.95.

Poems, mostly short, by some seventy women from thirty-eight countries in thirty-one languages, provide a "reflection of the concerns of women poets in our time." The poems are arranged by "recurrent themes": Being a Woman, Women and Men, Meditations, Speaking for Others, and Visions. Includes some well-known writers (Akhmatova, Hébert, Weil, Mistral), others less well known, and a few poems from oral traditions. The voices are crisp, vivid, and varied; "most [translators] have chosen to preserve the poetic image of the original poem within a clear and natural English" rather than trying to reproduce their prosody. Most pieces would be accessible to competent 10th grade readers and up.

157. Bankier, Joanna, and Lashgari, Deirdre, eds. ***Women Poets of the World***. New York: Macmillan, 1983. 416p. $12.95.

Almost 250 poets from China, Japan, the Arab world, the Middle East, ancient Greece, Africa, some dozen countries of medieval and modern Europe, and from the Native American, Afro-American, Asian/Pacific-American, Euro-American, and Chicana traditions of North America are represented in this collection, most by only one or two poems. No biographical information other than dates is given for the poets, but the ten introductions to the language groupings are very informative, discussing historical and sociological contexts as well as matters of prosody and imagery. There is not much overlap with **158** and **160**; even when the same poet is featured, the poems or the translations are almost always different. The strengths of this collection are the introductions, which are readable by competent

11th and 12th graders, and its broad coverage of minority women in the United States. Its weakness is that it gives no sense of an individual poet's range. Reading difficulty of selections varies; most are more suitable for older students.

158. Barnstone, Aliki, and Barnstone, Willis, eds. ***A Book of Women Poets, Book of Puzzlements: From Antiquity to Now.*** New York: Schocken Books, 1981. 640p. $12.95.

This anthology presents 788 poems by 311 poets, grouped chronologically within each language, from a Sumerian moon priestess born in about 2300 B.C. to nearly one hundred contemporary writers. Represented are works in eight Indian, eight Native American, six African, and three Arabic languages; from seven Spanish- and six French-speaking countries; in Welsh, Papuan, Polish, Hungarian, Chinese, Hebrew, and twenty other languages. Several works by most authors are featured; many of the same poets are included here as in **160** but only about one-fifth or fewer of the same poems appear in both books. There is little difference in the breadth or depth of the headnotes introducing each poet; **160** provides fewer selections for each individual, whose range and style can therefore better be seen in this volume. Separate indexes to poets, translators, titles, and first lines are included. At the high school level, some selections would be accessible even to slow readers, 9th grade and up.

159. Bulkin, Elly, and Larkin, Joan, eds. ***Lesbian Poetry: An Anthology.*** Watertown, Mass.: Persephone Press, 1981. 296p. $10.95.

Opening with a history of and introduction to lesbian poetry, this volume presents 145 poems written between 1919 and 1978 by 64 poets. Some of the writers are well known (Sarton, Rich), others less so; they are of various races, ethnic backgrounds, and social classes. While giving full weight to the political and pedagogical difficulties of teaching lesbian literature in a heterosexual setting even at the college level, the editors nevertheless affirm "the importance of taking risks in order better to understand the experiences and perceptions of women who [may] differ significantly" from the teacher and the student. Each must admit "her own fears, her own stereotypes, her own myths," and place them "within the framework of a society that has taught us homophobia." High school teachers might consider using selections by Tsui and Birtha, Bloch's "Six Years," Gordon's "When I Was a Fat Woman," Pratt's "My Mother Loves Women," Klepfisz's "They Did Not Build Wings for Them," Grahn's "A Mock

Interrogation," Allen's "Beloved Women," and Rich's "Phantasia." Pedagogical notes on teaching lesbian poetry conclude the volume.

160. Cosman, Carol; Keefe, Joan; and Weaver, Kathleen. ***The Penguin Book of Woman Poets.*** New York: Penguin, 1979. 399p. $5.95.

About 400 poems, "spanning 3,500 years and representing almost forty literary traditions," were chosen for representativeness as well as excellence. The poems are presented chronologically—an arrangement from which "suggestive similarities of genre and motif emerge." Headnotes of a paragraph or so give some information about each poet and her historical and literary contexts. This volume is deliberately light on contemporary poets, for more of whom see **156.** For larger selections of poems by many of the same authors, see **158.** The translations do justice to the originals, creating readable, and often fine, poems in English. Selectively useable with all students. There is twenty percent or less overlap in poems with **158.**

161. Fannin, Alice; Lukens, Rebecca; and Mann, Catherine Hoyser. ***Woman: An Affirmation.*** Lexington, Mass.: D. C. Heath, 1979. 439p. $12.95. *Instructor's Manual.* $1.95.

This book "developed from women's need to move beyond the stereotypes" to show that "women can surmount oppression and need not define themselves solely as satellites of men." Forty-six poems, twenty-four short stories, five folktales, five autobiographical sketches, and a play, selected for "excellent writing and strong woman protagonists," feature works by Behn, Dickinson, Woolf, Colette, Dinesen, Lessing, Lorde, Ling, and Rich, among others. A few are by men. Selections are grouped by "stages of a woman's life," and range from rhetorical appeals to philosophical statements, from anger at injustice to quiet self-respect. Subjects include struggle, choice, the recognition of limitations, exuberant joy, celebration of autonomy, and facing life's end with dignity. A "Rhetorical Table of Contents" groups selections under headings such as character, conflict, point of view, image, setting, tone, theme, diction, and rhythm. Study questions for each selection deal intelligently with matters of content, structure, and style. Most of the material is readable, with some help, by competent 10th graders and up.

162. Ferguson, Mary Anne, ed. ***Images of Women in Literature.*** 3d ed. Boston: Houghton Mifflin, 1981. 528p. $16.50.

Contains "31 short stories, 3 plays, and 29 poems that illustrate traditional images of women and also reflect the changes in those images brought about by the current women's movement and current serious scholarship about women. The images are organized in 7 categories linked to women's various roles in society." A 17-page introduction examines ideas about stereotypes as reinforced by archetypes, discusses the nature of common stereotypes about women, and reviews feminist scholarship in the various fields relevant to a countering of stereotypes. Selections, by both sexes, in Part I "exemplify the major stereotypes of women associated with their biological roles: those of mother, wife, sex object." Yet skillful reading, the author claims, will reveal a critique of the roles even in these works. Part II shows ways that women have sought to transcend the socially limiting stereotypes of their traditional roles. Each selection is headed by a photograph of the author and brief biographical notes. Includes an 11-page annotated bibliography. Selectively readable by competent 11th and 12th graders.

163. Folsom, Maria McClintock, and Kirschner, Linda Heinlein. ***By Women: An Anthology of Literature.*** Boston: Houghton Mifflin, 1975. 478p. $15.96. *Instructor's Resource Book.* 99p. $6.60.

Grouped by genre and topic, eighty-eight selections represent "the creative energies of women." Authors include the "familiar and not so well known," the classical (Sappho), and the contemporary (Wakoski, Oates.) Some selections have not been published in any other contemporary anthology. Lacking a theoretical framework and an overall introduction, each selection is introduced by a headnote that summarizes content rather than providing critical commentary. The questions for students that follow the selections are pedestrian and fact-oriented; the *Instructor's Resource Book* tends to belabor the obvious, though it does identify relative difficulty of the suggested readings. Intriguing illustrations in various media by both sexes, but the rationale for inclusion is often unclear. Useful for teachers who already have a solid background in the history and theory of women's literature and a well-thought-out course for which they could choose readings from the smorgasbord provided.

164. Gilbert, Sandra M., and Gubar, Susan. ***The Madwoman in the Attic: A Study of Women and the Literary Imagination in the Nineteenth Century.*** New Haven: Yale University Press, 1979. 733p. $16.95.

Has been called, and with good reason, "stunningly erudite." It is also ambitious, dense, and solidly argued. Having focused "closely on a number of 19th century texts we consider crucial," among them works by Jane Austen, Mary Shelley, Emily and

Charlotte Bronte, George Eliot, and Emily Dickinson, the authors "found what began to seem a distinctively female literary tradition." They describe it as characterized by "images of enclosure and escape, fantasies in which maddened doubles functioned as asocial surrogates for docile selves, metaphors of physical discomfort manifested in frozen landscapes and fiery interiors." The authors make the further claim that to understand literature by women, we have to understand the nature and origin of men's images of woman as "angel" and "monster." They establish that such images exist, and discuss how this influences women authors. Difficult but rewarding reading.

165. Hiatt, Mary. ***The Way Women Write: Sex and Style in Contemporary Prose.*** New York: Teachers College Press, 1977. 152p. $8.95.

This computer-aided study of one hundred works of fiction and non-fiction by male and female authors published between 1965 and 1975 finds that by objective criteria such as sentence length, sentence complexity, parallel constructions, rhetorical devices, and use of similes and adjectives, "the profile of women's writing is quite different" both from men's writing and from "the many hackneyed impressions of women's style." In the sample investigated, women were more terse and used shorter, less complex sentences; supported their arguments with reasons rather than, as did the men, with illustrations; and used more similes than did men in non-fiction, and a wider range of similes in fiction. Vocabulary analysis suggested that "women intuit considerably more often than the men, but do not reason proportionately less often"; for single words, the only significant difference was that only women used the adjective "lovely." The author concludes that women writers were "moderate in tone, well balanced, rational, organized and 'unextreme' "; their writing "reflects a more varied perception of the world" than the men's; and "their style embraces more varied syntactic structures." Because of methodological reservations concerning the derivation of the sample used, it would be dangerous to generalize on the basis of this study, which is nevertheless a provocative one. Students could easily duplicate the research design in miniature and would probably be interested in exploring it, with or without a computer.

166. Hoffman, Nancy, and Howe, Florence, eds. ***Women Working: An Anthology of Stories and Poems.*** Old Westbury, N.Y.: The Feminist Press, 1979. 271p. $9.95.

Thirty-four selections from the 1700s through the 1960s "explore the emotional texture of women's work," paid and unpaid, among colonial, frontier, immigrant, black, Hispanic, Native American, and working-, upper-, and middle-class women. Selections, some by the well known such as Cather, Giovanni, and Rich, and a few by men, are grouped under the headings Oppressive Work, Satisfying Work, Family Work, and Transforming Work. A sixteen-page introduction discusses the nature of women's work, presents a brief history of it, and identifies recurrent literary themes. Headnotes of a paragraph or two give biographical information about the authors, whose portraits serve as illustrations. Thoughtful and well-crafted. Developed for high school use; good for average 10th to 12th grade readers. The *Teaching Guide* by Florence Howe and Alexandra Weinbaum (72p., $5.00) provides historical and literary background, classroom strategies, and teaching suggestions that deal with issues such as sexist and black language, point of view, genre, and themes, as well as content. Useful eleven-page annotated bibliography includes films.

167. Juhasz, Suzanne. ***Naked and Fiery Forms: Modern American Poetry by Women, a New Tradition.*** New York: Harper & Row, 1976. 212p. $3.95.

This study focuses on the textual analysis of poetry written by nine women, from Dickinson and Moore to Giovanni and Rich. The author seeks to establish that a new tradition of women's poetry, characterized by "a voice that is open, intimate, particular, involved, engaged, committed," now exists; and to document its emergence. She does so by drawing knowledgeably, intelligently, and elegantly on psychological, sociological, historical, biographical, and textual analysis. Includes a four-page bibliography.

168. Kaplan, Sydney Janet. "Review Essay: Literary Criticism." ***Signs*** 4, no. 3 (Spring 1979): 514–27.

Topics covered are women and the literary tradition, women poets and novelists, and feminist criticism.

169. Moffat, Mary Jane, and Painter, Charlotte, eds. ***Revelations: Diaries of Women.*** New York: Random House, 1975. 411p. $4.95.

Of literary, historical, and psychological interest, these diary excerpts span several centuries and many countries. The thirty-two writers, aged seven to eighty, some obscure and some famous, include Dorothy Wordsworth, Louisa May Alcott, Käthe Kollwitz, Marie Bashkirtseff, and an unknown Japanese woman. Their work is arranged under the headings of Love, Work, and Power. Part of the editors' intent was to "see if it was possible to define the diary . . . as a valid literary form," as well as being a reflection of women's social circumstances and individual inner lives. Headnotes of a page or so provide contexts for the excerpts. More suitable for older students, though some would appeal even to 9th graders. Interesting comparisons may be made with **123.**

170. Moore, Honor, ed. ***The New Woman's Theater: Ten Plays by Contemporary American Women.*** New York: Random House, 1977. 537p. $6.95.

A useful introduction gives a twenty-six-page history of women as playwrights, from Hroswitha, a tenth-century Saxon nun whose plays celebrate Christianity but who also used "rape as a metaphor for male sin and the oppression of women," to the 1970s. The authors represented by their plays write about female experience, which they have chosen to place in the theater—some from a wry distance, others with a fierce and disturbing immediacy or with painful humor. One is explicitly a play for children, in the Eskimo idiom; another, a dramatization of history that "bring[s] our foremothers to life." Selectively useable with students; some explicitly sexual language.

171. Phelps, Ethel Johnston. ***The Maid of the North and Other Folk Tale Heroines.*** New York: Holt, Rinehart, 1981. 192p. $6.25.

These twenty-one traditional folk and fairy tales, representing seventeen different ethnic cultures from around the world, "portray spirited, courageous heroines," a "surprisingly rare" species. Most of the tales "follow the story outlines of earlier sources quite closely," but have been "retold with . . . freedom," including addition and omission of details. Intended primarily for elementary grades, but the easy to read stories have potential student interest at the 9th and 10th grade levels. They provide a good basis for student discussions about sex roles and the images of women and men in literature. Slow readers may need help with some of the vocabulary. Includes attractive black and white illustrations.

172. Pratt, Annis. ***Archetypal Patterns in Women's Fiction.*** Bloomington: Indiana University Press, 1982. 224p. $6.95.

Based on works of more than 300 British and American novelists both "major" and "minor," and including working-class, black, and lesbian writers, the author finds that "women's fiction reflects an experience radically different from man's because our drive towards growth as persons is thwarted by our society's prescriptions concerning gender. . . . The disjunction between the author's social conscience and her need for selfhood renders characterization ambivalent, tone and attitude ambiguous, and plots problematic." She sees the principal recurrent archetypes of women's fiction as "the green-world epiphany, the green-world lover, the rape trauma, enclosure, and rebirth"; and their expression as providing "a ritual experience for the reader containing the potential for personal transformation." Although there is little extended discussion of individual novels, the book offers the possibility of fresh insight into any novel, which teachers could share with students whatever the reading list happens to consist of; especially so since the author found that "women's shared experience as women endows their fiction with a degree of continuity, abundance of analogue, and uniformity of concern sufficient to elucidate a single work by reference to the field of the woman's novel as a whole." Useful sixteen-page bibliography lists novels and stories, books and articles on feminist literary theory, and works on authors.

173. Register, Cheri. "Review Essay: Literary Criticism." ***Signs*** 6, no. 2 (Winter 1980): 268–82.

Feminist criticism is examined as "one of several sets of skills that scholars bring to . . . the illumination of 'female experience.'" Some of the topics considered are the feminist canon, the question of a female aesthetic, the mother-daughter focus, and the female mythos.

174. Sargent, Pamela, ed. ***The New Women of Wonder: New Science Fiction Stories by Women about Women.*** New York: Random House, 1978. 363p. $3.95.

Eleven stories by some well-known (McIntyre, Tiptree, Russ) and some less-known writers present female characters in nontraditional roles. The stories raise questions about sex-role assumptions, the relationships between women and men, how men see women, how women see themselves, and the possibilities for radical change. Several of the stories would make excellent bases for thoughtful student discussions. Recommended for competent 10th grade readers and up.

175. Shimer, Dorothy Blair, ed. ***Rice Bowl Women: Writings by and about the Women of China and Japan.*** New York: New American Library, 1982. 390p. $4.50.

These thirteen stories from China, half written after 1911, and nine from Japan, half written after 1868, span the period from 600 A.D. to the present. A useful introduction clearly explains the basic philosophical and social concepts necessary for an understanding of the stories. Headnotes give information about historical setting, customs, and conditions, as well as about the authors. Some of the stories are short enough to be read in the classroom. The collection is valuable not only for its subject matter, but also because it allows comparisons of literary conventions within each of the two countries at different times, between the countries, and between each country and the West. For competent readers.

176. Showalter, Elaine. ***A Literature of Their Own: British Women Novelists from Bronte to Lessing.*** Princeton: Princeton University Press, 1976. 378p. $9.95.

The author argues for the existence of a "female literary tradition in the English novel" that comes "from the still-evolving relationship between women writers and their society." She identifies three overlapping stages: Feminine, from the 1840s to 1880, when there was imitation of the dominant (male) tradition and internalization of its standards; Feminist, from 1880 to 1920, with protest against the former tradition and advocacy of women's own values and rights; and Female, after 1920, characterized by the search for identity and self-awareness. The thirty-three-page introduction provides a helpful, concise historical overview of writers and their work since about 1750. Appealing and readable even for the interested nonspecialist. Biographical appendix of the 213 "most prominent literary women born in England after 1800" is a bonus reference feature.

177. Sternburg, Janet, ed. ***The Writer on Her Work.*** New York: W. W. Norton, 1981. 265p. $6.95.

This volume consists of seventeen essays by American women novelists, poets, and non-fiction writers from various backgrounds, including Bambara, Jong, Kingston, Ruckeyser, and Walker. They discuss how they began writing, who and what influenced them, the texture of their daily lives, and the necessary choices they have made and continue to make as women and artists. The essays "deliberately reflect on the creative process," "suggest that multiple choices are possible," and argue that "against the fragmentation caused by conflicting demands . . . various parts of the self can nourish one another." The four- to twenty-page essays vary from the elegantly lean and witty to the angry, discursive, and tersely matter-of-fact. Reading level varies; recommended for average 9th graders and up.

178. Washington, Mary Helen, ed. ***Black-Eyed Susans: Classic Stories by and about Black Women.*** Garden City, N.Y.: Doubleday, 1975. 200p. $4.50.

A collection of ten stories about growing up black and female, relationships between mothers and daughters, women and men, black and white women, and the tyranny of white ideals of physical beauty. The twenty-two-page introduction shows how "the authors of the stories in this collection . . . have broken through the old myths and fantasies about black women," and because of them, "there are more models of how it is possible for us to live," from the teenager in a sharecropping family "who had a way of springing back from pain" to the mother who feels that it "ain't like I'm old old." On the whole, the tone of the stories is muted, and they show the influence of the past rather than the promise of the future (for which see **179**). For competent 11th and 12th grade readers.

179. Washington, Mary Helen, ed. ***Midnight Birds: Stories of Contemporary Black Woman Writers.*** Garden City, N.Y.: Doubleday, 1980. 274p. $4.95.

The fifteen stories in this collection focus on relationships between women, between women and men, and on the quest for identity. Stylistically more complex and less immediately accessible to most adolescents than those in **178,** they add up to a sturdier collection, with protagonists "more open to adventure, prouder, more strong-minded, more defiant." An introduction sets out the main issues and themes of the selections; headnotes introduce authors and their works, often largely in the authors' own words.

180. Webber, Jeannette L., and Grumman, Joan. ***Woman as Writer.*** Boston: Houghton Mifflin, 1978. 451p. $17.50.

Works by over two dozen well-known writers of the twentieth century, including black and working-class women, are grouped into those making "statements about the creative process [in] journals, essays, poetry and fiction . . . in order to show what writing means to the writers"; and the "results of the creative process," from the novels, short stories, poetry, drama, and essays of the same writers. While the book as a whole focuses on the creative process, the selections themselves span "a wide spectrum of women's experiences: initiation, relationships with women and men, motherhood, work, aging." The collection includes at least two works by each writer, which together "present a chronological view of the women writing in England, Canada and America in the 20th century."

Speaking in voices of fantasy, anger, bitterness, irony, and humor, the overall tone of the selections is upbeat. Headnotes introducing each author are concise, vivid, and informative about both life and work. An interesting idea, well executed, and very useful to the teacher of creative writing. Useable with competent or better 11th and 12th grade readers.

HISTORY

TEACHING METHODS AND THEORY

181. Alpern, Mildred. "Images of Women in European History." ***Social Education*** (March 1978): 220–24.

Concise and informative discussion of some of the revisions to be made, and questions to be asked, in teaching about the Renaissance, Liberalism, the Enlightenment, and twentieth-century European art in light of the new scholarship on women's history. Set in the practical context of questions asked on the Advanced Placement examination. High school level.

182. Chapman, Anne. "Placing Women in the High School European History Survey." ***The History Teacher*** 12, no. 3 (May 1979): 337–47.

Suggests "ways to incorporate women's history into the basic European survey course by giving examples of specific content, classroom techniques, and resources that teachers can use to develop their own approaches." Periods discussed in some detail are the Middle Ages, Renaissance, Enlightenment, Industrial Revolution, and twentieth-century Russia.

183. Chapman, Anne, ed. ***Approaches to Women's History.*** Washington, D.C.: American Historical Association, 1979. 143p. $5.00.

Seven curriculum units oriented toward social, family, and quantitative history, biography, sex-role socialization, and the inquiry method present substantial content about U.S. women's history of the nineteenth and twentieth centuries. More than fifty brief, interest-provoking documents are included—poems, statistics, science fiction, manifestos, sermons, cartoons, houseplans, and excerpts from sociological and medical writings. Units on Sex Roles, Family History, Women's Rights, Work in and out of the Home, and Biography each have detailed lesson plans, extensive discussion questions, and innovative activities promoting student involvement on both analytic and emotional levels, and the simultaneous learning of subject matter and skills. The annotated resource list of 126 items is keyed to the units and geared to the expansion of the curriculum. Best with competent 10th and 11th graders, but easily adaptable for younger and older students. Interdisciplinary, versatile, and crammed with information, this book is useful both for those new to the field and for those looking to expand their knowledge.

184. Fox-Genovese, Elizabeth, and Stuard, Susan Mosher, eds. ***Restoring Women to History: Materials for Western Civilization.*** Vol. 1. Bloomington, Ind.: Organization of American Historians, 1983. 355p. $15.00. OAH, 112 North Bryan Street, Bloomington, Ind. 47401.

Fifteen curriculum units emphasize "gender as a primary distinction in historical experience." The units range from "Prehistory: Hunters" through "Classical Greece," "The Renaissance: The Commercial Revolution and the Urban Medieval Family," "The Age of the Baroque: Monarchs and Philosophers," to "Challenges to the Old Regime" in the eighteenth century. Each unit suggests concepts and subject matter for several lectures, reading assignments for students, topics for discussion, audiovisual aids, and a bibliography for instructors. Thought-provoking and dense. Volume 2 is forthcoming. College level.

185. Jeffrey, Kirk, and Cirksena, Diane. "Women's History in the High School Survey: An Integrationist Approach." ***The History Teacher*** 11, no. 1 (November 1977): 39–46.

An introduction to the subject for those with little or no previous acquaintance with it. Contains brief suggestions for specific ways to integrate women's history into colonial, revolutionary, and progressive reform periods. Sources cited in notes largely superseded; those in text still useful.

186. Lerner, Gerda. ***The Majority Finds Its Past: Placing Women in History.*** New York: Oxford University Press, 1979. 217p. $7.95.

Twelve essays by one of the leading pioneers and practitioners of women's history. In this book, Lerner offers a historiography of women's history; calls into question the appropriateness of traditional periodization when considering women; and stresses "the need for separate consideration of class, race and ethnicity in analyzing women's past." Lerner distinguishes between "the woman's rights movement," aimed at achieving equality for women within male-defined society, and "feminism," the "struggle for female autonomy and self-determination." She argues that "women's unpaid household work [is] a primary causative factor . . . in her general subordinate status" and offers a "radical critique of traditional history" as a step toward creating "a new 'universal history' . . . in which men and women will have equal significance." Includes three chapters on black women. Keen thought embodied in lean and sinewy prose. This is mind-stretching reading.

187. Lerner, Gerda. ***Teaching Women's History.*** Washington, D.C.: American Historical Association, 1981. 88p. $5.00.

This pamphlet by a leading scholar tries "to provide an overview of the new field of women's history; . . . to discuss the methods and techniques for teaching the subject, with particular attention to interdisciplinary approaches; . . . to meet the needs of those wanting to incorporate women's history into existing survey or topic courses and of those wanting to teach separate units of courses on the subject; and to give an introduction to primary and secondary sources and to the bibliographies in the field." In all this it succeeds admirably, and, in addition, provides a useful historiography of women's history; a list of "teaching questions designed to bring women into view"; and suggestions for topical approaches, such as women-focused family history, the housewife in the economy, and woman suffrage. For each topic, Lerner outlines the major issues, gives substantive information about them, and reviews the literature. There are sections on the uses of autobiography and biography, and on women of racial and ethnic minorities. Focusing on North American material, the approaches, questions, and pedagogical suggestions are adaptable to almost any history course. Incisive, invigorating, and indispensable, this practical manual should be top-priority reading for both neophytes and pros.

188. Pleck, Elizabeth; Fox-Genovese, Elizabeth; Wilson, Joan Hoff; and Woodman, Harold, eds. ***Restoring Women to History: Materials for U.S. History.*** Vol. 2. Bloomington, Ind.: Organization of American Historians, 1984. 666p. $20.00. OAH, 112 North Bryan Street, Bloomington, Ind. 47401.

Individual curriculum units structured to fit traditional periodization start with "The Reconstruction," and end with the

1970s. Format and approach resemble that of **184**, also by the OAH. Volume 1 is expected in the near future.

189. ***Women's History 1984 Curriculum Guide.*** Santa Rosa,, Calif.: National Women's History Week Project, 1984. 71p. $7.50.

Designed for use by elementary and secondary level educators "unfamiliar with the history of women," this well-intentioned but skimpy volume provides neither substantive nor theoretical grounding in the subject. The dozen or so miscellaneous projects, activities, and discussion questions it features for the high school level are neither thought-provoking nor specifically rooted in the realities of women's history. They include writing a news release about a historic event in the women's rights movement, a poster-making contest, a research project, and a bulletin-board display. Includes an almost exclusively biography-oriented "potpourri of women's historic accomplishments" in question-and-answer form; six biographies of two to three pages each with study questions; a couple of "dramatic enactments"; and a personal/family history questionnaire. The bibliography of student readings has uncritical annotations, is almost exclusively biographical, and is not uniformly reliable. A somewhat better, if idiosyncratic, selection of teacher resources includes some audiovisual materials. If used, the *Guide* should definitely be reinforced and supplemented by more thorough sources.

UNITED STATES HISTORY

Narrative Surveys

190. Banner, Lois W. ***Women in Modern America: A Brief History.*** New York: Harcourt Brace Jovanovich, 1974. 276p. $11.95.

A narrative survey from 1890 to the early 1970s, this book explores "why feminism rose and fell and rose again"; examines the "history of the working class, blacks, immigrants, farm women and the middle class," each of whom responded to the pressures and opportunities of the times in a different way; and describes the struggle for women's rights. Plain, sturdy prose; attractive format and design; the more than one hundred crisp, striking illustrations are a valuable resource in themselves. Though becoming dated, the annotated bibliographies following each chapter are still useful. Accessible to competent 11th and 12th grade readers.

191. Hymowitz, Carol, and Weissman, Michaele. ***A History of Women in America.*** New York: Bantam, 1978. 400p. $4.50.

A narrative history for the general reader, this book draws on the recent historical scholarship on women. The authors aim to "strike a balance between the lives of average women and . . . extraordinary women," and between "women's experience . . . as a document of oppression" and women's creation of "meaning, purpose, beauty and dignity in their lives despite the limitations placed upon them." Vividly and perceptively written, the skillfully woven story gives due allowance to the diversity of class, race, and geographical area, and is liberally laced with quotations from primary sources. Lends itself to chapter-by-chapter assignment as parallel and comparison to the conventional textbook. For good 10th, competent 11th and 12th grade readers; a bargain. This and **190** are the best narrative texts for older students; **193** for younger.

192. Matthaei, Julie A. ***An Economic History of Women in America: Women's Work, the Sexual Division of Labor and the Development of Capitalism.*** New York: Schocken Books, 1983. 384p. $11.95.

Interested not in a compilation of facts (although it provides a wealth of vividly concrete information), but in the principles and processes that gave rise to them, this book focuses "on the family, the economy, and their interface." In the colonial period, it covers family economy, homemaking, husbandless women's work for income, and slave labor in and out of the family; in the nineteenth and early twentieth centuries, the development of separate spheres and the "cult of domesticity," the "working girl," and homemaking as a profession; in contemporary North America, the creation of sex-typed jobs, marriage, and career (from either/or to both/and), and the breakdown of the sexual division of labor in and out of the home. A reading of this absorbing narrative is likely to result in the development of a new slant on the teaching of the U.S. history survey course. Sensitive to issues of race, class, and ethnicity, and challenging in its ideas, the book is written in incisive, vigorous prose punctuated by numerous quotations of a paragraph or more from primary sources, and by twenty-five tables.

193. Millstein, Beth, and Bodin, Jeanne. ***We, the American Women: A Documentary History.*** Rev. ed. Chicago: Science Research Associates, 1983. 363p. $12.67.

A textbook for high school students that spans the period from colonial times to the 1970s, this chronologically arranged survey is well illustrated, attractive, and substantial. It includes a lucid and informative text and approximately one hundred well-chosen documents, including excerpts from diaries, letters, manifestos, poems, biographies, reminiscences, cartoons, and statistics. In each chapter, the authors explain the general legal and social status of the women in that period, describe the contributions of various outstanding women to the shaping of the nation at that time, and analyze "the roles played by the 'average woman' as a force in maintaining society and pressuring for change." Less satisfactory are the separate, elementary *Activity Book* (64p. $2.73) and the *Teacher's Guide* (44p,, $2.14) with routine discussion questions, projects, and an annotated bibliography. Appropriate for 9th grade readers and up.

194. Norton, Mary Beth. "Review Essay: American History." ***Signs*** 5, no. 2 (Winter 1979): 324–37.

Concentrating on articles, this essay covers work on various aspects of nineteenth-century, middle-class, white women's lives; on the "dark ages" of the 1920s to the early 1960s; and debate on the status of colonial women.

195. Sanders, Beverley. ***Women in American History: A Series.*** 4 vols. Newton, Mass.: Education Development Corporation, 1979. $10.00.

Covering the period from 1609 to 1920, these volumes are developed specifically for use in high schools to accompany the standard history survey. The series seeks to balance "famous" and "ordinary" women. The rather pedestrian prose of the text is enlivened by copious, telling quotations from primary sources. Shows awareness of changes in historical interpretation (as in views of the black family), and of diversity in the lives and experiences of women due to race, class, or geographical location. The Inquiry Questions following each chapter depend heavily on factual recall; the suggested activities are unimaginative. For average to better 9th to 12th grade readers. A good selection for those not interested in using primary documents with younger students.

Collections of Essays and Documents

196. Downey, Matthew T., ed. ***Teaching American History: New Directions.*** Washington, D.C.: National Council for the Social Studies, 1982. 115p. $7.25.

Chapter 1, "The 'New World' of Women's History," contains a ten-page summary of recent research and thoughts about its significance by a major scholar, a bibliographical essay, and descriptions of four different classroom exercises developed by high school teachers. These are: constructing an "attic trunk" as evidence of women's lives in a particular period, writing obituaries to show different expectations and life experiences of the sexes and changes therein over time, debating the topic of women's suffrage, and analyzing women's work in the twentieth century through use of statistical tables. This last exercise includes suggestions on ways to use statistics in the classroom that are widely adaptable. An easy introduction to the field of women's history and some of the opportunities it offers for teaching at the high school level.

197. Friedman, Jean E., and Shade, William G., eds. ***Our American Sisters: Women in American Life and Thought.*** 3d ed. Lexington, Mass.: D. C. Heath, 1982. 448p. $13.95.

Twenty-seven essays, most by well-known scholars, are organized here into four chronological periods, each headed by an introduction "that outlines the major unifying themes of the period and relates the essays to the themes." Each section includes material on society's definition of women's proper roles, the actual conditions of women, and women's response to those conditions. Several essays deal with the differential effects of region, class, race, religion, and ethnicity on women's lives. Topics include the planter's wife, divorce in eighteenth-century Massachusetts, the dynamics of interracial sex, religion in the Victorian era, working-class women in the Gilded Age, sisterhood and conflict in the Women's Trade Union League, black women and the Great War, and women in the Kennedy Administration. Provides a great deal of worthwhile and useful information, regrettably often couched in unwieldy prose. Virtually no overlap with **202** or **199,** both of which are better sources for the nonspecialist.

198. Hellerstein, Erna Olafson; Hume, Leslie Parker; and Offen, Karen M. ***Victorian Women: A Documentary Account of Women's Lives in England, France, and the United States.*** Stanford: Stanford University Press, 1981. 544p. $11.95.

An alternative to the "traditional approach that has fitted women's experience into preconceived structures of historical change and periodization," this collection of 106 documents is drawn from diaries, letters, advice manuals, and medical, legal, and government records, often previously unpublished, and structured "around the stages of the female life-cycle" from birth to death. This organization "confronts readers with the Victorian vision that biology was destiny and asks them to grapple with the issue of biological determinism." The collection allows an exploration of the relationship between ideology and lived experience, between image and reality. It includes both unknown and exceptional women of diverse classes and geographical areas. It raises the questions: "Is there a female experience that transcends class, culture and ethnicity?" How did the social relations between the sexes change and how did they remain the same during the nineteenth century? Introductions of a dozen or so pages to each section give a historical context to selections dealing, among others, with childhood on a rural French estate, life in an English boarding school, courtship in America, contraception, slave motherhood, infant care among the working class, and the rituals of death. Reading difficulty of selections varies; most are accessible to students of varying abilities and ages.

199. Katz, Esther, and Rapone, Anita, eds. ***Women's Experience in America: A Historical Anthology.*** New Brunswick, N.J.: Transaction Books, 1980. 414p. $7.95.

A valuable source for bringing together a number of highly influential historical essays. The sixteen readings, including "The Lady and the Mill Girl," "The Cult of True Womanhood," and "The Female World of Love and Ritual," cover various topics in colonial, nineteenth-, and twentieth-century societies, from Anne Hutchinson to nurses in the Union army, settlement houses, family limitation, the Overland Trail, flappers, and career women. The editors' revisionist introduction criticizes the stress that has been placed on women's economic roles as a key factor in explaining their changes in status. They argue that the nineteenth-century separation of home and work was a positive development for women; that the domestic culture and ideology "provided a foundation for the extension of women's activities" into the public world; and that, with its breakdown in the twentieth century, "integration into the male world became imperative," but remains unachieved. For readers new to women's history, it would be helpful to read **187** first.

200. Katz, Jonathan, ed. ***Gay American History: Lesbians and Gay Men in the USA.*** New York: Avon, 1978. 690p. $3.95.

Nearly one hundred documents from a paragraph to a few pages long are presented in six chronologically arranged topical sections:

Trouble, 1566–1956; Treatment, 1884–1974; Passing Women, 1782–1920; Native Americans/Gay Americans, 1528–1976; Resistance, 1859–1972; and Love, 1779–1932. Extensive bibliographies follow each section. In selecting lesbian materials, "special attention was paid to those documents which reflect on issues raised by the recent women's liberation and Lesbian-feminist movements" and those that "permit the authentic voice of a speaker to come through."

The material assembled documents the experience of "ordinary gay people." Among the sources included are records of churches, universities, and insane asylums; articles in medical, psychological, psychiatric, and legal journals; court records; ephemera of the early American homosexual emancipation movement; reports by governments, missionaries, explorers, and anthropologists; references in artistic and literary works; excerpts from biographies, autobiographies, and diaries. Some of the documents have not previously been published. Introductions to each section and brief headnotes to each selection serve to set the context. Intended for "general readers of all sexual persuasions," the book, already a classic, also intends to present the material "most useful to gay women and men in our present struggle to create a positive, rounded sense of self, to establish unalienated ways of relating, and to abolish those social institutions that deny us." Reading difficulty of the documents varies; their suitability for high school use should be individually weighed by teachers.

201. Katz, Jonathan Ned, ed. ***Gay-Lesbian Almanac: A New Documentary.*** New York: Harper & Row, 1983. 764p. $16.30.

This book presents some 350 documents from a wide variety of sources, a number of them previously unpublished, including excerpts from autobiographies, letters, legal statutes, trial records, medical writings, reviews, editorials, songs, cartoons, and photographs. They are arranged in chronological order to "help situate homosexual history precisely in a particular society at a specific stage of development." Stress is on the documentation of oppression and resistance, especially in the context of the contrast between the colonial "Age of Sodomitical Sin, 1607–1740" and the modern world's "Invention of the Homosexual, 1880–1950." About half of the documents are identified as "containing the most substantial references to women-loving women." The evidence is analyzed in two essays that precede the two sections; a general introduction discusses "some theoretical and practical problems . . . in defining, researching and interpreting lesbian and gay American history."

202. Kerber, Linda K., and Mathews, Jane DeHart, eds. ***Women's America: Refocusing the Past.*** New York: Oxford University Press, 1982. 478p. $13.95.

The three major chronological sections of this anthology, which includes some sixty articles and documents, are "generally congruent with familiar periodization": i.e., traditional, industrializing, and modern North America. The editors see the complex interaction over time of biology, economics, politics, and ideology as "crucial to understanding women's differing historical experience." Each section includes articles by major scholars in each of these four categories, accompanied by primary source documents and an introduction that pins down the issues touching women at the time and relates them to what is usually taught about the period. Selections include both biographical and statistical approaches, and vary from the abstract and theoretical to the concrete and personal; some of the most specialized pieces are also the most intriguing ("Household Technology and Social Change," "Smothered Slave Infants: Were Slave Mothers at Fault?" "Women, Civilization and the Indian Question"). A clear, concise, and judicious essay, "The New Feminism and the Dynamics of Social Change," gives a very useful, up-to-date summary of the historical background, origins, development, ideas, and impact of the women's movement, noting internal problems as well as external opposition. Best for those who already have some background in the subject; some of the selections could be assigned to competent 10th grade readers and up. Includes a seven-page annotated bibliography.

203. Lerner, Gerda, ed. ***The Female Experience: An American Documentary.*** Indianapolis: Bobbs-Merrill, 1977. 509p. $14.47.

Using a thematic historical organization that establishes a "new framework for the study of women's history," this book focuses on the life cycle, experiences, and self-definition of ordinary women. Ninety-one documents present primary source material ranging from childhood in slavery to nursing an aging mother, the school marm, collective bargaining for household technicians, voting for school boards in Ohio, a female soldier in the American Revolution, consciousness raising, and women's search for autonomy. Helpful fifteen-page introduction provides context and theoretical background; headnotes give biographical and historical information for each selection as well as pointers on their significance. Reading difficulty varies; most could be assigned, selectively, to 9th grade students and up.

204. Tetreault, Mary Kay Thompson. ***Women in America: Half of History.*** Chicago: Rand McNally, 1978. 240p. $8.80.

This collection of over seventy documents, including excerpts from autobiographies, readers, memoirs, letters, law codes, petitions, and poems has been designed specifically for high school students. Arranged topically, the documents cover socialization of girls by the family, the media, and schools; marriage and singleness, homemaking, childrearing, and growing old; and volunteer work for service and for change, wage work, and careers. A chronological index groups the documents into five historical periods; over one-third are from the 1970s. Headnotes give a context for each section; briefer notes give the background to each document, followed by thoughtful questions and activities for students. Reading difficulty varies; suitable for competent 9th graders and up. A well-chosen selection for high schools, but it is advisable for teachers to have some background in women's history before using it. (Good places to start: **183, 186, 187, 196.**)

205. U.S. Bureau of the Census. ***A Statistical Portrait of Women in the U.S.*** Washington, D.C.: Bureau of the Census, Current Population Reports: Special Series P–23, no. 58, 1976. Available from the U.S. Government Printing Office. 90p. $2.10.

This topical arrangement of eighty-six tables into fourteen chapters, each with a brief introduction summarizing highlights, gives information on "the changing role of women in the U.S. during the 20th century." Some of the time series start in 1900, most in 1950 or even later. The analyses provide information on population growth and composition, longevity, mortality, health, residence and migration, family and marital status, fertility, work participation and experience, income, voting and public office holding, and crime and victimization. Some data on black and Hispanic women is given. Useful as background information for teachers, and, in the classroom, not only as illustration for generalizations but as raw material for hypothesis-building in inquiry-oriented exercises. Also useful for comparisons with descriptions of "the changing role of women" in textbooks, and with relevant literary sources. For ideas on using statistical data with students, see **196.**

206. Wertheimer, Barbara Mayer. ***We Were There: The Story of Working Women in America.*** New York: Pantheon, 1977. 427p. $8.95.

Arranged chronologically, this book chronicles the experiences of Native Americans, slaves, colonials, pioneers, trade unionists, teachers, and factory, clerical, garment, mill, and mine workers up to World War I. Filled with vivid detail, it combines statistical with anecdotal information, and lively stories about individuals with institutional histories. It is more descriptive and less analytical than **108** and treats a broader range of women workers. The sturdy prose of the text is studded with substantial (a paragraph to a page or more) excerpts from primary sources. Selectively assignable to competent 11th and 12th grade readers.

Works That Focus on a Single Period or Locale

207. Brown, Dee. ***The Gentle Tamers: Women of the Old Wild West.*** Lincoln: University of Nebraska Press, 1981. 335p. $6.50.

While this continues to be included in current bibliographies, it is to be avoided even though its flamboyant style has student appeal. Gratingly jocular and patronizing in tone, it leans toward the sensational (rapes by Indians, massacres, "Ladies of Easy Virtue"). The insistence on "petticoat pioneers," "feminine daintiness," and woman's eagerness to "display her charms to the best advantage," is not adequately balanced by chapters on "A Home in the West," "Wyoming Tea Party," and "Casting off the Shackles."

208. Faragher, John Mark. ***Women and Men on the Overland Trail.*** New Haven: Yale University Press, 1979. 304p. $8.95.

Important as one among the so far pitifully few attempts at "the creation of a history of women and men in their real connectedness," this study is based on 169 diaries, letters, and written recollections, about half from each sex. The narrative describes, in sturdy prose, the Midwestern farming family (typical of those journeying West); the "separate worlds" of the sexes (though the author concludes that "these women and men were part of a common culture" and were "more alike than different"); "masculine men and feminine women"; and the "world of the Family." Liberal use is made of quotations, both from the letters and diaries and from ballads and songs of the period, most of which could be assigned to students of various reading abilities. Fourteen tables provide demographic data; a six-page "Notes on Method" could usefully be read by able 11th and 12th graders to see a historian at work. The twenty-eight-page bibliography is arranged by genre and topic.

209. Green, Harvey, and Perry, Mary E. ***The Light of the Home: An Intimate View of the Lives of Women in Victorian America.*** New York: Pantheon, 1983. 256p. $8.95.

Based on a study of surviving artifacts, nineteenth-century advice literature, and nineteenth-century fiction, this book describes the domestic lives of unexceptional middle-class women of the urban and village northeast in America during the period of about 1870 to 1910. Chapter topics include courtship and marriage, motherhood, housework, home decorating, health, leisure, and death. With no theory or analysis, this is a straightforward account in plain prose with occasional excerpts from original sources, dealing with rarely touched-on topics: children's toys, wedding etiquette, exercise, mourning ritual, etc. Good as a source for comparisons between the nineteenth and twentieth centuries. Could be selectively assigned to competent 11th and 12th grade readers; the 122 unusual contemporary illustrations, showing styles in clothing and coffins, pictures of nursing bottles and kitchen tools, advertisements for childrens' corsets and pessaries, are a resource in themselves.

210. Hartman, Susan M. ***The Home Front and Beyond: American Women in the 1940's.*** Boston: Twayne, 1982. 235p. $15.00.

Dealing with "women in the aggregate" rather than with "the unique activities or contributions of individual women," this study tries "to encompass the experiences of women across class and racial lines" and pays "much greater attention to the public sphere than the private domain." Starting with a "survey of the major developments in American political, economic, and social life during the 1940's," the author goes on to consider women in the paid labor force and in the army; women's education; women's status in the political, legal, and family systems; and the role models available to women in popular culture. Offers a lot of detailed information rather than analysis, with much citing of statistics and frequent brief quotations from primary sources. Includes a six-page bibliographic essay. Karen Anderson's *Wartime Women: Sex Roles, Family Relations, and the Status of Women During World War II* (Westport, Conn.: Greenwood Press, 1982, 198p., $8.95) is more steeped in academese and has a narrower focus.

211. Jeffrey, Julie Roy. ***Frontier Women: The Trans-Mississippi West 1840–1880.*** New York: Hill & Wang, 1979. 256p. $7.25.

A detailed narrative examination of "many frontiers—farming, mining, Mormon—to which women reacted differently." Shows the diversity of white women's experiences during the continental expansion of the United States—not bounded by, but relevant to, the Turner Thesis. Based on over 200 women's journals, reminiscences, letters, and some interviews, the author concludes that, contrary to her expectations, pioneer women did not use "the frontier as a means of liberating themselves from stereotypes and behaviour which I found constricting and sexist," but she understands why they did not. Both the ideology and the reality of women's experience is shown, from the wearing of gloves to handle the buffalo dung used for fuel to the terse comment, "I keep close to my gun and dog." The text is scholarly and reasonably readable, and contains brief quotations from primary sources. The chapter on Mormons conveniently presents information hard to find elsewhere.

212. Kerber, Linda. ***Women of the Republic: Intellect and Ideology in Revolutionary America.*** Chapel Hill: University of North Carolina Press, 1980. 304p. $8.95.

Stimulating and authoritative, this study focuses more on the minds and actions of women than on how they felt about their lives. The lucid text is interwoven with many vivid quotations from original sources of a few words to half a page ("If She did not fight she threw in all her mite which bought the Sogers food & Clothing & Let them have Blankets"). It covers female patriotism (typically consisting of the expectation "to suffer, to admire the military, and to maintain her innocence"), "the loyalties that married women owed to the state," divorce, education, and the redefinition of female political behavior as valuable (if peripheral) rather than abnormal. The author concludes that the Revolution did not much affect the prevailing ambivalence toward women's education, though it had an impact on divorce law. For many women the Revolution had been a "strongly politicizing experience"; women's search for "a political context in which private female virtues might comfortably coexist with the civic virtue . . . regarded as the cement of the Republic" resulted in the notion of "Republican Motherhood," a dedication "to the nurture of public spirited male citizens," which "had the advantage of appearing to reconcile politics and domesticity."

213. Levine, Suzanne Braun, ed. ***She's Nobody's Baby: A History of American Women in the 20th Century.*** New York: Simon & Schuster, 1983. 224p. $12.95.

Based on a Peabody Award-winning documentary, this collection of photographs, posters, and cartoons (many of them rare archival material), is arranged by decade. Connected by a minimal yet informative text that combines statistics, biography, social trends, significant dates, and telling quotations, this would be a worthwhile source for inquiry-oriented classes, slow readers, and supplementary assignments at the high school level.

214. Lord, Sharon B., and Patton-Crowder, Carolyn. ***Appalachian Women: A Learning/Teaching Guide.*** Newton, Mass.: Education Development Center, 1979. 184p. $6.00.

For general format, see **70.** This guide is divided into four units that deal with Appalachian women in music and literature, contemporary and historical sex roles and role models, work, and health and education. The readings provided (some are only referred to) vary from those readable with interest by competent 9th graders to those to be conscientiously waded through by a dedicated teacher. Lesson plans, discussion questions, and activities are detailed and thoughtful. Includes a twenty-six-page annotated list of media resources and bibliography. Some of the material could be adapted for use in teaching about other rural regions.

215. Luchetti, Cathy, and Olwell, Carol. ***Women of the West.*** St. George, Utah: Antelope Island Press, 1982. 240p. $17.00.

A "document of personal experience" rather than "academic history," this impeccably produced book offers "a sense of life as lived by western women between 1840 and 1915." The text is comprised of eleven carefully edited sets of journals, letters, and diaries, including those of a Paiute translator for the U.S. army, a school teacher, a French Catholic nun, a middle-class black widow, the owner of a large cattle ranch, a Mormon handcart pioneer, and a divorced physician. In styles ranging from the florid to the terse, the literary to the barely literate, women talk uninhibitedly of their concerns. Two introductory chapters, one on minority women, give historical background. The 140 arresting contemporary photographs of "women actually doing things," from branding cattle to soliciting, sharing housework with husbands, teaching, riding, and driving a team of oxen are remarkable for being multiethnic, technically good, and unusually informative. A valuable resource for slow readers; excerpts from the text also could be assigned to most students, 9th grade and up.

216. Norton, Mary Beth, ed. ***Liberty's Daughters: The Revolutionary Experience of American Women, 1750–1800.*** Boston: Little, Brown, 1980. 384p. $10.95.

Based on the papers of some 450 eighteenth-century families, Norton's cogently argued text is enlivened by quotations from letters, diaries, poems, and other writings by women both black and white on a wide variety of topics. Comments from original writings range from "I hope I shall have no more for indeed I get very weakly with nursing and bearing children," to "I have Don as much to Carrey on the warr as meney thatt Sett Now at ye healm of government & No Notice taken of me." Norton concludes that women were not, as has been contended, "relatively equal partners"; that most "denigrated their sex in general"; and that, contrary to previous belief, "the Revolution had an indelible effect" on them, both boosting their self-image and men's respect—results that were embodied in educational reform. Her interpretation of women's progress after the Revolution is, however, disputed by other scholars. The division of chapters into topic-oriented, relatively self-sufficient sections would make it easy to assign these to students who are good readers in the upper high school grades. The eleven-page essay on sources is heavily research oriented.

217. Ruether, Rosemary Radford, and Keller, Rosemary Skinner, eds. ***Women and Religion in America, Volume I: The 19th Century.*** San Francisco: Harper & Row, 1982. 368p. $10.53.

In seven chapters, women's role and experiences in revivalism, Utopian movements, immigrant Catholicism, the Jewish and the Protestant traditions, and in social reform movements are examined. While recognizing "the repressive, isolating and negative influence of religion" and its role in reinforcing "piety, domesticity and submissiveness . . . as essential to women's nature," the authors see "religion as an infinitely variable instrument for 'enlarging women's sphere.'" Each chapter includes an analytical essay and a set of illustrative documents including letters, pamphlets, autobiography, and journal articles. The approach is historical rather than theological or mystical. Some of the documents could be assigned to competent 11th and 12th grade readers.

218. Schlissel, Lillian. ***Women's Diaries of the Westward Journey.*** New York: Schocken Books, 1982. 272p. $16.95.

Based on a study of over one hundred women's diaries, the

author "believes that the two sexes saw the overland trek with different eyes." Women's views may be explained, in part at least, by the fact that 20 percent of them were pregnant and almost all of them responsible for small children at the time of the trip west, which "the great majority of the women did not want to make" in the first place. On the trail, women "were often called upon to do chores recognized as men's work," but they intended "to restore the domestic sphere as soon as possible." In their "steadfast clinging to ribbons and bows, starched white aprons and petticoats," women kept reasserting their traditional "social role and sexual identity." Over half the book consists of vigorous prose narrative and clear-headed analysis, laced with excerpts from various diaries, including those of some black and single women. The balance of the text reproduces three diaries and a memoir "just as they were written," though slightly abbreviated. Selectively readable even by slow 9th graders. The forty-eight archival photos are heavy on formal portraits, but some show striking details of daily life.

219. Spruill, Julia Cherry. ***Women's Life and Work in the Southern Colonies***. 1938. Reprint. New York: W.W. Norton, 1972. 464p. $7.95.

A classic from 1938, this impeccably intelligent work written in lucid, flowing prose is a gold mine of information. The author writes about "the everyday life of women, their function in the settlement of colonies, their homes and domestic occupations, their social life and recreations, the aims and methods of their education, their participation in affairs outside the home, and the manner in which they were regarded by the law and by society in general." Quotations from primary sources contribute to the vivid pictures presented of housewives and their helpers, tavern hostesses and planters, shopkeepers and artisans; of wardrobes, ladies' libraries, and girls' schooling; of "conjugal felicity" and domestic discord, being "in the increasing way," and legal status. Selected passages or even chapters could be assigned to able 11th and 12th grade readers. The twenty-seven-page bibliography is a good guide to original sources.

220. Ulrich, Laurel Thatcher. ***Good Wives: Image and Reality in the Lives of Women in Northern New England, 1650–1750***. New York: Knopf, 1982. 296p. $17.50.

Based on the evidence of captivity narratives, court records, account books, probate inventories, gravestones, embroideries, and the private papers of husbands and sons, the author characterizes each of her subjects as having been "simultaneously a housewife, a deputy husband, a consort, a mother, a mistress, a neighbor, and a Christian," who might also, "on the war-torn frontier," become a heroine. The deftly written text, dealing with economic life, sex and reproduction, and with captives, resisters, and "viragoes," is interwoven with quotations from primary sources, and gives excellent insight into the homely details of women's (and men's) lives. Descriptive rather than analytical. The thirty-five black and white illustrations help visualization.

221. Wandersee, Winifred D. ***Women's Work and Family Values, 1920–1940.*** Cambridge: Harvard University Press, 1981. 192p. $18.50.

This book argues that, in this period, the majority of working women as well as homemakers were still committed to a traditional pattern of family life. While acceptance of "the dual role of the employed housewife" was related to the "concept of 'companionship' in marriage" and to an improvement in women's status within the family, feminism "suffered a major setback during the interwar years because it refused to recognize the continued importance" of family life and values to most North American women. The book's six chapters combine a chronological with a topical approach, and are strongly statistical while also drawing on literary sources. The author examines the economics of family life, the Depression's effects on income and standard of living, demographic trends, the experience of working women, and women's place in the home. There is more consciousness of class than of race issues. The text is scholarly but not overly technical. The twenty-four statistical tables could be used in the classroom (for suggestions on ways to do so, see **196**). Includes an eight-page topical bibliography.

222. Ware, Susan. ***Holding Their Own: American Women in the 1930s.*** Boston: Twayne, 1982. 223p. $15.00.

"The role of the Depression in shaping American culture and society in the 1930's molds this book," which "surveys developments in fields as diverse as popular culture, employment, and sexuality," as well as education, feminism and social reform, women on the Left, literature, and the fine arts. The topical treatment, descriptive rather than theoretical, combines statistical and biographical information with brief quotations from both primary and secondary sources. The result is somewhat bland of taste and lumpy of texture, but neither difficult nor boring to read; and it does offer a lot of detailed information as well as suggesting the overall interpretation that women both suffered less from the Depression than did men and, by working, helped to bring about recovery. Includes ten tables and a ten-page bibliographic essay.

EUROPEAN HISTORY

Narrative Surveys

223. Branca, Patricia. ***Women in Europe Since 1750.*** New York: St. Martin's Press, 1978. 233p. $25.00.

A scholarly narrative history that describes and interprets changes in women's work and family roles from preindustrial society to the mid-twentieth century, with a focus on England and France and scattered references to other European countries. It treats less thoroughly education and political activity. Emphasis is on social, economic, and demographic trends rather than on individual women or events. More of a broad overview than **111,** which gives a better idea of the diversity existing within each country at a given time. A six-page bibliography, almost entirely of secondary sources, directs the reader to more detail on specific topics.

224. McKay, John P., and Hill, Bennett D. ***A History of Western Society.*** 2d ed. Boston: Houghton Mifflin, 1982. 1,072p. $27.95.

None of the standard European history textbooks is adequate, let alone satisfactory, when it comes to the treatment of women. This one is the least inadequate. Having made "social history the core element" of their work, the authors present a fairly substantial body of information about women's education, family and work roles, sexuality (childbearing, rape, prostitution, birth control), and life cycle, starting with the ancient Near East through the 1960s—albeit usually under a separate heading of "women." Illustrations show not only the obligatory upper middle-class mother at family dinner, but women in a sweatshop and setting firebombs during the Paris Commune. The suggested readings include works on women's history, a field with which the authors are evidently familiar. Written in plain, clear, forceful and sometimes lively prose, each chapter starts with basic questions and ends with a summary. The book neither spoonfeeds nor overwhelms; it gives telling detail and avoids trivia; includes some spirited biographical sketches; quotes "rather extensively from a wide variety of primary sources," hardly any of them by women; and could be used in honors courses with able 11th and 12th graders. The *Study Guide* (294p., $6.95) is competent but unimaginative, containing a synopsis, outline, and fact-oriented "discussion" questions for each chapter.

225. Steiner, Shari. ***The Female Factor: Women in Western Europe.*** Chicago: Intercultural Press, 1983. 328p. $12.95.

A "contour map" of women and their influence in England, Italy, France, Germany, and Scandinavia, this book looks at history, archetypes, statistics, expert opinions, and at "how women felt and behaved in their offices, supermarkets and homes." It deals with socialization, paid work, housekeeping, love, motherhood, and images of women. Much of the research rests on interviews with authorities and ordinary individuals, combined with the author's own thirteen-year experience as a journalist in Europe. Couched in flowing prose spiced with brief quotations, it gives a lot of detailed, useful, and interesting factual information. While often flippantly superficial in its generalizations ("the Italian feels that the woman is essential and the male accessory; the Anglo-Saxons perceive woman as a second-class man; the French believe she is a different species"), it is the only convenient, readable comparative overview of contemporary European women's position.

226. Stephenson, June. ***Women's Roots: Status and Achievements in Western Civilization.*** Napa, Calif.: Diemer-Smith, 1981. 128p. $9.95.

Unacceptable because of the author's total lack of acquaintance with the new scholarship on women, and, it would seem, with historical scholarship in general. She makes unqualified claims (as for prehistoric matriarchy) that are at best controversial and at worst incorrect. She relies uncritically on idiosyncratically chosen, outdated, and obscure "authorities"; and the information she presents is repeatedly questionable, misleading, and sometimes just plain wrong. Only twenty-five pages deal with the whole of the post-1400 period; and the topics she chooses to cover are unbalanced (e.g., of six paragraphs on pre-nineteenth-century slavery, five are an excerpt from a secondary source describing the voyage to America).

Collections of Essays and Documents

227. Bell, Susan Groag, ed. ***Women: From the Greeks to the French Revolution.*** Stanford: Stanford University Press, 1980. 313p. $7.95.

Originally compiled in 1970, some thirty selections from both original sources (St. Jerome, Margaret of Angoulême) and secondary works (Carcopino, Power, Burkhardt) aim to illustrate "the lives of women and men's views of women." Each of seven chronological divisions is introduced by a headnote that "sets the historical stage," and individual readings are headed by "a few paragraphs that indicate their significance." Topics covered range from Roman priestesses and matrons to medieval nunneries and trading women, courtly love, female Renaissance scholars, salonnières, and working women in the French Revolution. While still of some use to those looking for additional readings, since the compilation of this book a lot of new information and new interpretations about the history of women has been generated. Students are likely to find the ponderous prose a stumbling block to enjoyment, if not to understanding.

228. Bell, Susan Groag, and Offen, Karen M., eds. ***Women, the Family, and Freedom: The Debate in Documents.*** Vol. I, 1750–1880. 561p. $14.95. Vol. II, 1880–1950. 474p. $13.95. Stanford: Stanford University Press, 1983.

This collection of 264 documents by authors mostly from England, France, and Germany, and by both well-known and less-known women and men, is arranged chronologically and topically. Substantial essays introduce each of the six major periods covered, presenting considerable background information, identifying major issues, and sketching national, class, and ideological differences. Each of the 100 or so sets of documents is preceded by a useful one-to-two-page headnote that provides the historical context and suggests the significance of the writings; each set emphasizes the "debate" theme by featuring both prevailing and dissenting views about a given topic at a particular time. Topics touched on range from woman's nature and position in family and society, to education, law, work (both blue collar and professional), political rights, and political action. Documents include excerpts from law codes, newspaper articles, reports on congresses, parliamentary debates, and the writings of philosophers, psychologists, sociologists, politicians, reformers, historians, and literary figures. Accessible even to people without much expertise, it would be most useful for those having some acquaintance with the field. Just reading through the introductions and headnotes is worthwhile.

229. Bridenthal, Renate, and Koonz, Claudia, eds. ***Becoming Visible: Women in European History.*** Boston: Houghton Mifflin, 1977. 510p. $15.50.

Geared to the "needs of a college audience using standard historical works," and organized chronologically, the twenty chapters by different contributors include "Women's Egalitarian Societies," "The Pedestal and the Stake: Courtly Love and Witchcraft," "Did Women Have a Renaissance?" "Women in the Age of Light," "Love on the Tractor: Women in the Russian Revolution," and "Mothers in the Fatherland: Women in Nazi Germany." Brief headnotes pinpoint the main issues for each chapter. Written by specialists, in scholarly but unpretentious prose, these straightforward and stimulating essays cover economic, political, social, and cultural history. Probably still the best choice for any classroom teacher committed to incorporating material on women into a survey course, or to teaching a unit or elective in European history. Suggested further readings tend to be technical.

230. Murray, Janet Horowitz. ***Strong-Minded Women and Other Lost Voices of Nineteenth-Century England.*** New York: Pantheon, 1982. 417p. $11.95.

This collection of over 150 primary readings, 34 of them by men, tells the story of middle- and upper-class women's "struggle to escape the confinement of home," working-class women's struggle "to ensure her own and her family's survival," and "women's collective effort to redefine the boundaries and potentialities of the womanly life." "The women speak about their families, their sexuality, their work, their friends, their sorrows and their achievements," and consider also "the nature of womanhood itself." A thirteen-page introduction provides historical context. The editor is sensitive to differences in the experiences of classes, between the popular imagery and the realities of women's lives, to changes during the century, and to the role of religion both as a source of antifeminist ideology and a means whereby women transcended the limits of their lives. Selectively assignable to almost any student readers from grade 9 up. The forty or so thought-provoking and visually striking contemporary illustrations are a resource in themselves.

231. O'Faolain, Julia, and Martines, Laura, eds. ***Not in God's Image: A History of Women in Europe from the Greeks to the Nineteenth Century.*** New York: Harper & Row, 1973. 305p. $6.95.

Several hundred excerpts from contemporary documents cover classical Greece and Rome, Byzantium, Islam, and Europe from the Middle Ages to the 1850s. The book "aims at presenting a close-up picture of the lives of ordinary women of different social classes: of their status, social roles, degrees of freedom or tutelage, and of the mental conditioning which has survived to leave its residue in attitudes of our own time." Editorial comments set the brief (from a few lines to a few paragraphs) readings into historical context and try to bridge gaps. Selections are from diaries, letters, laws, memoirs, poetry, manuals, and sermons; most are by men, the majority from before 1600. Suffers from having been compiled in 1970, before most of the theoretical work in women's history had been done, but is still useful as a convenient compendium that can be selectively assigned to students from slow 9th grade readers to honors seniors. The twenty-five striking and provocative illustrations are a resource in themselves. The three-page bibliography should be used with caution, if at all.

232. Riemer, Eleanor S., and Fout, John C., eds. ***European Women: A Documentary History, 1789–1945.*** New York: Schocken Books, 1980. 251p. $7.95.

Under headings of "Work," "Politics," "Family," and "Woman and her Body," fifty-three documents "present the thoughts of women who lived in West and Central Europe and Russia." A few are by the famous, "but most are the words of unrenowned, 'average' women," taken from pamphlets, journals, broadsides, and periodicals "written . . . by women, for women." Although they represent "working-class as well as middle—and to a lesser extent, upper class women," each selection "illustrates experiences common to women across Europe." They touch on such varied topics as the hard conditions in Russian factories, the opening of the German civil service "as a respectable branch of business to ladies," the forced feeding of imprisoned suffragists in England, and "the fetters of motherhood" in Austria. Introductions to each chapter and to each document give substantial historical information, identify major issues and trends, provide biographical details, and make cross-references to other documents in the collection. Good for inquiry-oriented courses and supplementary readings; many selections are accessible even to slow 9th grade readers, though some students will need help with concepts and issues. Includes a fourteen-page bibliography.

Works That Focus on a Single Period or Locale

233. Abray, Jane. "Feminism in the French Revolution." ***American Historical Review*** 80, no. 1 (February 1975): 43–62.

Gives a brief account of women's status under the *ancien régime;* of feminist theory and activity during the Revolution; of feminist leaders and their ideas; of attitudes and actions concerning women of the revolutionary governments; and discusses the reasons for the failures of revolutionary feminism.

234. Atkinson, Dorothy; Dallin, Alexander; and Lapidus, Gail Warshofsky, eds. ***Women in Russia.*** Stanford: Stanford University Press, 1977. 410p. $9.95.

Eighteen essays by historians, political scientists, sociologists, anthropologists, and economists cover historical background, sex roles and social change, and women in law, politics, and education. In an excellent, concise chronological account, from the legendary Amazons and Kievan Russia up to the twentieth century, one essay considers women within political, social, and intellectual contexts. Other essays deal with factory workers, the intelligentsia, and Marxism; equality in Soviet policy; rural, industrial, and professional working women; the equal pay issue; and an analysis of men and women in children's readers that invites comparison with similar U.S. data (a comparison that, with research assistance, students could be assigned to perform themselves). From the nineteenth century, when female nihilists "by the score bade farewell to parents, husbands and even children and fled their gentry nests" looking for personal and sexual freedom, to the twentieth, when rural girls six years of age worked fourteen-hour days in factories, and women were losing out in the higher professional ranks "primarily [because of] the negative impact on women's productivity of their home responsibilities," a clear picture of women's lives emerges. The scholarly prose, more heavyhanded in some essays than in others, is studded with a number of instructive tables.

235. Bingham, Marjorie Wall, and Gross, Susan H. ***Women in the U.S.S.R.: The Scythians to the Soviets.*** Hudson, Wis.: Gary E. McCuen, 1980. 123p. $4.95. From the Women in World Cultures Series; for their common features see **260.**

Developed for high school use, to be "blended in to already existing curriculums." Sensitive to issues of class and ethnicity, and leaning only slightly toward the "great women" approach, the easy-to-read narrative text follows a chronological arrangement. The focus throughout is on the interplay between control and change, and on how women effected and were affected by each. Each section (e.g., "Olga: Kievan Hero"; "Red Virtue to Soviet Family") is liberally laced with quotations from original sources, and is followed by questions to students that are generally thought-provoking yet rooted in the text. Includes maps, charts, chronological tables, and glossary.

236. Bogin, Meg. ***The Women Troubadours.*** New York: W. W. Norton, 1980. 192p. $4.95.

Fifty-six page introductory essay (which has been criticized by scholars) looks at the history of southern France from the eleventh to the thirteenth centuries, tracing the rise of commerce, changes in law, effects of the crusades, and women's role and status. It also suggests a new interpretation of courtly love: "the veneration of the lady was indeed a break with both the classical and early Christian traditions," but it was still "essentially a system men created with the dreams of men in mind"; and "to consider this development a positive one for women would be to ignore its crippling effect" down the centuries, to our own day. The essay goes on to the *trobairitz* themselves, the twenty known noble women poets, eighteen of whom are represented here, and whose "language and the situations they describe are strikingly different from those of their male counterparts." Two to three poems are included by each *trobairitz* in the original Provençal with smooth and occasionally colloquial translations on facing pages: "Now don't start yakking, young girl . . . I have a mind to ask about another friendship if you don't shut up," and "as for me, I'm much improved, although for you I have no use." Liberally illustrated with black and white reproductions of contemporary art and photographs of the castles where the *trobairitz* lived, the book offers a new slant on a significant aspect of the Middle Ages.

237. Glückel of Hameln. ***The Memoirs of Glückel of Hameln.*** Translated by Marvin Lowenthal. New York: Schocken Books, 1977. $7.95.

This diary of a forty-four-year-old German Jewish widow with fourteen children, begun in 1640, tells in flowing, spirited colloquial prose not only about her own life as a pillar of her family and a successful businesswoman, but of the Jewish community's affairs and of the wars that touched her. She records personal triumphs and sorrows—drafting the contract when her husband entered a partnership; giving birth at the same time as her mother and mixing up the babies; and fleeing "fairly naked all the way to Hamburg" when, "everything being frozen, the Swedes overran the country." A fascinating tale that is like a window opened onto a segment of the late seventeenth-century world. The nine contemporary illustrations help visualization. Excerpts are readable by competent 10th graders and up.

238. Kanner, Barbara, ed. ***The Women of England from Anglo-Saxon Times to the Present: Interpretive Bibliographical Essays.*** Hamden, Conn.: Shoe String Press, 1979. 429p. $30.00.

Much more than a bibliography, this work suggests topics and often substantive information that can be woven into survey courses. Four articles on the Middle Ages, one on early modern England (1485–1714) and two each on the eighteenth, nineteenth, and twentieth centuries review sources and subjects. "Each author has selected a set of questions . . . appropriate and significant for the historical period and sociocultural context," and pursues them through "a critical evaluation of primary and secondary references," while suggesting "how the findings may be employed in teaching." Subjects covered include women in medieval law, eighteenth-century social history, Victorian demography, and the nineteenth-century novel as a historical source. While some background in the discipline would be helpful, the book is readable even by the nonspecialist.

239. King, Margaret L. "The Religious Retreat of Isotta Nogarola (1418–1466): Sexism and Its Consequences in the Fifteenth Century." ***Signs*** 3 (Summer 1978): 807–22.

Case study detailing the experiences of a female humanist. Considers the historical setting.

240. Lapidus, Gail Warshofsky, ed. ***Women, Work and the Family in the Soviet Union.*** Translations by Vladimir Talmy. Armonk, N.Y.: M. E. Sharpe, 1982. 356p. $14.95.

Unusual in being "a selection of the best recent Soviet writings on these subjects in translation," this collection is meant to illustrate the problems, present the findings of recent research, and "offer a glimpse of current policy debates." In addition to dealing with educational and skill levels in industry, protection of female labor, maternal care of infants, women in agriculture, demography, changing family roles, and how women combine work with household duties, the seventeen articles also give a lot of incidental information about social conditions and the Soviet economy as a whole. Nearly fifty tables invite comparison with U.S. data, and lend themselves to analysis in the classroom. (For suggested techniques, see **196.**) The somewhat ponderous prose is stuffed with figures but is not hard to read. Six appendixes give excerpts from key Soviet legislative documents relevant to the topics covered.

241. Levy, Darline Gay; Applewhite, Harriet Branson; and Johnson, Mary Durham, eds. ***Women in Revolutionary Paris, 1789–1795.*** Urbana: University of Illinois Press, 1979. 325p. $10.00.

This collection of sixty documents is organized "chronologically to demonstrate changes in women's political awareness and tactics." Materials include the fishwives' homage to the Third Estate; a petition to the National Assembly by over three hundred women for "permission to procure pikes, pistols and sabres . . . and to practice maneuvers" with them; the Paris laundresses' protest to the Convention that the price of bleach had risen "so high that soon the least fortunate class of people will be unable to have white underwear, which it cannot do without" and request of the death penalty for hoarders; and the convention's outlawing of women's societies to avoid women's neglect of "the more important cares to which nature calls them." Taken together, the four- to six-page introductions to each of the six chronological sections provide an overview of women's political roles during the period. Some documents could be assigned to students; they are not so much difficult, as often laborious, to read.

242. McMillan, James F. ***Housewife or Harlot: The Woman Question in France under the Third Republic.*** New York: St. Martin's Press, 1981. 229p. $27.50.

Did French women in the Third Republic, although explicitly subordinate to men by law, in fact enjoy "power and influence behind the scenes"? What was "the nature, extent and practical relevance of [the] ideology of domesticity," and to what degree was the "doctrine of separate spheres" challenged by the rise of feminism? Was motherhood "the instrument of women's oppression or of their progressive emancipation"? How did women's economic activity (or inactivity) relate to their status? These and other questions are tackled, based on evidence mostly from urban women predominantly from the Paris region, and with careful attention to differences between the experiences of middle- and working-class women, to demographic and legal data, family structure, educational opportunities, and female participation in the labor force. The "framework of sex discrimination," marriage, sex and the family, education and employment, and feminism are examined in the prewar period. So are women's experience in, support of, and opposition to, the war;

the social impact of the war; and the fate of feminism as well as "the durability of the double standard" after the war. Refreshingly outspoken in defense of his own interpretations, the author provides insight into the lives of women during the period. For more recent material on French women, see **225.**

243. Moses, Claire Goldberg. ***French Feminism in the Nineteenth Century.*** Albany: State University of New York Press, 1984. 311p. $12.95.

Starting with a useful summary of the history of the "woman question" in France before 1800, the author goes on to relate the legal, economic, and social condition of women to feminist thought in the next century. She concludes that the discontinuity of feminism was tied "to the political fluctuations of French history," and especially "to the fate of the political left," with interruptions due to repressive governments. Feminists responded to the changing realities of women's experience by changing their focus and their program. For instance, early Saint-Simonian advocacy of free love was abandoned on finding that this led to hardship because of women's inability to support themselves and their children in a society where men were not legally responsible for the support of their illegitimate offspring, and women were both poorly paid and lacked access to training for better paying jobs. Later, when the "ideology of motherhood extolled female virtues," feminists "built on the respect accorded women as mothers to demand . . . equal rights" for them. While it was only in the last decades of the century that feminists scored a number of legislative victories, the author claims for the earlier utopians an influence greater than their numbers suggested. They "transformed [for the better] the Romantic attitude towards women," and had an effect on the thinking of Mill, the Grimkés, Anthony, and Butler. The detailed analysis of utopian ideas, including a tracing of changes due to both personal and public circumstances, is based on extensively cited excerpts, many from letters. Dealing as it does with working-class and bourgeois women, and with the realities of women's lives as well as political context and feminist thought, this is a useful volume for teachers. Includes an eleven-page research-oriented bibliography.

For a very different and more narrowly focused view, see Bonnie G. Smith's *Ladies of the Leisure Class: The Bourgeoises of Northern France in the Nineteenth Century* (Princeton: Princeton University Press, 1981, 303p. $11.50), "a case study [of] a group of women who lived in the department of the Nord," which suggests that "although physically part of an industrial society, bourgeois women neither experienced its way of life nor partook of its mentality." Having accepted their relegation to a largely reproductive function in society, they created their own, separate world centered on domesticity, family, and religion. Reading both volumes gives a sense of the diversity of women's experience and concerns.

244. Pomeroy, Sarah B. ***Goddesses, Whores, Wives and Slaves: Women in Classical Antiquity.*** New York: Schocken Books, 1976. 280p. $7.95.

This clear, well-balanced, reliable narrative history of women in ancient Greece and Rome, from about 1184 B.C. to 337 A.D., is based on evidence from tombstones, coins, graffiti, household objects, inscriptions, and charms as well as legal documents, literary evidence, and the writings of ancient historians, biographers, orators, and philosophers. It tries to avoid "emphasis on the upper classes," and to give an impartial account of the heated debates about prehistoric matriarchy, the status of citizen women in Athens relative to slave women and citizen men, and the divergence between "women in actual society and the heroines on the stage." It succeeds. In doing so, it presents a lot of fascinating information: life expectancy estimates in classical Greece (forty-five for men, thirty-six for women); an account of prostitutes ("the only women in Athens who exercised independent control over considerable amounts of money"); the misogyny of classical literature; the Augustan legislation exempting women with three children from legal male guardianship; and that in imperial Rome "it was not unusual for the daughter of a lowly plebeian centurion to attend elementary school in the Forum," nor for women to write electoral endorsements in the form of graffiti. The sturdy, straightforward prose is sprinkled with quotations from a sentence to a page in length from original sources, mostly in pleasingly unstilted translations. The nine-page bibliography leans to the technical, and the nineteen illustrations are pedestrian.

245. Pore, Renate. ***A Conflict of Interest: Women in German Social Democracy, 1919–1933.*** Westport, Conn.: Greenwood Press, 1981. 152p. $25.00.

Informative on women as socialists, feminists, politicians, workers, wives, and mothers in the Weimar Republic. Statistics and quotations help show that the period "did not witness the liberation of women, but there was some progress, probably as much or more than in any other nation." Good source of background information for the teacher. Includes an eleven-page bibliography.

246. Power, Eileen. ***Medieval Women.*** Edited by M. M. Postan. London: Cambridge University Press, 1976. 144p. $6.95.

Based on popular lectures by a great medieval scholar and edited posthumously by another, this is a crystal-clear account of medieval ideas about women. It gives a good sense of medieval women's experience, including the lady, the working woman in both town and country, the education of women, and nunneries. Includes some excerpts from original sources. The forty-two striking and crisp illustrations can serve as excellent teaching aids. The text is accessible to competent or better 11th and 12th grade readers.

247. Quataert, Jean H. ***Reluctant Feminists in German Social Democracy 1885–1917.*** Princeton: Princeton University Press, 1979. 310p. $33.00.

Written in ponderous prose, with a barrage of detail and bristling with notes, the saving grace of this work is its feminist orientation (which is lacking in the other two studies on this topic: Richard J. Evans's *The Feminist Movement in Germany 1894–1933* [London: Sage, 1976], and Werner Thonessen's *The Emancipation of Women: The Rise and Decline of the Women's Movement in German Social Democracy 1863–1933* [London: Pluto Press, 1973]). It covers the historic connection of class and sex in Germany; woman as "work horse, Baby Machine, Cultural Drudge" in imperial times; the lives and work of eight socialist feminists, including Ihrer, Zetkin, and Braun; the socialist vision of work, marriage, and motherhood; institutional aspects of organization; party and union relations; women's socialist education; and the wartime divisions in the movement. Overall, too many trees and too little forest, but it's the best on this period and topic.

248. Robertson, Priscilla. ***An Experience of Women: Pattern and Change in Nineteenth-Century Europe.*** Philadelphia: Temple University Press, 1982. 673p. $14.95.

A narrative history with a social-intellectual focus on "the middle and upper segments of society" in England, Germany, France, and Italy, from roughly 1875 to 1914. The book is organized into two parts: "the pattern women's lives were expected to follow," centering on the marriage relationship; and "breakers of that pattern," which covers education, work, legal, and political issues and the feminist movement. The author "follows no regular order for dealing with the different countries," but focuses on that nation in which the topic being dealt with "was most coherent or dramatic, and then contrast[s] this one with the others." Recurring motifs are the increasing individualism of women, connected with their increasing participation in education and work; the structure of authority within the family; and the continuing, ambivalent relationship between the women's movement and socialism. Based exclusively on literary sources, descriptions of the way of life of the majority are balanced by thumbnail sketches of individual women and anecdotal illustrations: Mrs. Gaskell was "a versatile lady indeed, for whom, we are assured, household cares were a positive delight, who trained a succession of first-rate cooks, and who was prouder of her pigs than of her literary triumphs." Scholarly and somewhat overwhelming, but written in lucid prose that prevents it from being a chore to read. The mass of intriguing detail illuminates rather than clouds the clarity of its generalizations.

249. Rogers, Katharine M. ***Feminism in Eighteenth-Century England.*** Urbana: University of Illinois Press, 1982. 300p. $18.95.

Against an outline of the social and intellectual background of the first two chapters is set an examination of "diverse expressions of feminism in early women writers," of sentimentalism and radicalism in literature, of the feminine novel, and of how women saw themselves at the end of the century. Gives a useful, though because of its focus, one-sided insight into the period. The appendix lists over one hundred women writers in Britain between 1660 and 1800, and sketches the "factors that may have inhibited or encouraged their achievement: socio-economic background . . . relationship with parents, education, political and religious beliefs, means of support, literary friendships, and family circumstances."

250. Rothchild, Sylvia, ed. ***Voices from the Holocaust.*** New York: New American Library, 1982. 456p. $8.95.

Nearly 100 accounts, about half by women, detail life before, during, and after the Holocaust. Selected from among 250 taped memories of survivors in America, these stories of people from a dozen different European countries, mostly of middle-class backgrounds, give a vivid, compelling, and often heartrending picture of life in Europe on the eve of, and during, World War II. They tell of "the Holocaust that blew through their lives like a tornado"; of their survival, and the deaths of so many, during "Hitler's occupation of

Europe in beleaguered ghettos and concentration and slave labor camps"; of their activities as "partisans who fought in the forests and Zionists who made the dangerous and illegal journey to Palestine"; and of "their early struggle, their adjustments and accomplishments in America where they came as refugees." Accounts run from a couple to a dozen pages in length; a headnote gives brief biographical data for each. Competent 9th grade readers and up could handle most of the material; in classes with diverse ethnic backgrounds, assigned accounts could match student origins. Those wishing to delve more deeply will want to look at Vera Laska, ed., *Women in the Resistance and in the Holocaust: The Voices of Eyewitnesses* (Westport, Conn.: Greenwood Press. 330p. $29.95), drawn from diaries, autobiographies, and narratives.

251. Shaffer, Harry G. ***Women in the Two Germanies: A Comparative Study of a Socialist and a Non-Socialist Society.*** New York: Pergamon Press, 1981. 256p. $29.00.

"Equal rights provisions were incorporated into the 1949 constitutions" of both East and West Germany. In the former, the ideology of Marxist-Leninist thought was committed to such equality, whereas in the latter there was no such ideological commitment. The East has legislated extensive reverse discrimination; the West has not. Yet, in neither country has complete equality of the sexes been fully realized. This study covers women's position "under the law, in education, on the job, and in the home," and is based on information gleaned from official agencies, extensive interviews (primarily with women), as well as on reading. Some of the fine-print detail on, for example, pension supplements or types of day care gets tedious, but on the whole, this is a lucid and persuasive case-study with a lot of interesting and relevant information. Includes forty tables. For a more popular work on contemporary German women, see **225**.

252. Smith, Hilda L. ***Reason's Disciples: Seventeenth-Century English Feminists.*** Urbana: University of Illinois Press, 1982. 270p. $18.95.

Most immediately useful are the first two chapters, dealing with social and intellectual background. These reveal a "pattern of relative deprivation," where women's lives were not improving at the same rate as men's; greater limitations on women's thought in the English Renaissance than is usually claimed; and the relationship of feminist ideas to revolutionary ideology. Followed by a study of fourteen feminists, who, though they "did not have a lasting impact on the lives of women in the following century or a direct influence on feminist writings of the future," are important as pioneers in their "realization of women's group identity."

253. Stites, Richard. ***The Women's Liberation Movement in Russia: Feminism, Nihilism, and Bolshevism, 1860–1930.*** Princeton: Princeton University Press, 1978. 464p. $16.50.

"Descriptive narrative is balanced with biographical portraiture and a running analysis" in this book. It spans a period from the days of the convent, "a time-honored Russian method of dealing with refractory women," and of Parish schools, "whose principal mission was to transform daughters of priests into future brides of priests," to the heroine of the Revolution, who, "restless, and intoxicated by power, strapped on a Mauser and took up a post as head of the intelligence section of the Volga Fleet," and to our own day when "most Russian women are convinced that although work does not automatically confer liberation, true liberation is impossible without it." Important for the sake of comparison with Western feminism, and as a case study of the difficulties occurring in the translation of ideological commitment to equality into practical reality. More engagingly written than most monographs, this work is already regarded as a classic.

254. Thomis, Malcolm I., and Grimmett, Jennifer. ***Women in Protest 1800–1850.*** New York: St. Martin's Press, 1982. 166p. $25.00.

A descriptive account of the part played by (mainly working-class) women in food riots, social and industrial protests, and political reform movements, especially Chartism, in early nineteenth-century England. The information, presented in unpretentious prose with occasional brief (a paragraph or so) excerpts from original sources, could easily be incorporated into standard accounts of nineteenth-century English history—and should be.

AFRICAN HISTORY

255. Gross, Susan Hill, and Bingham, Marjorie Wall. ***Women in Africa of the Sub-Sahara.*** Vol. I. ***Ancient Times to the 20th Century.*** 143p. $6.95. Vol. II. ***The 20th Century.*** 117p. $6.95. Hudson, Wis.: Gary E. McCuen, 1982. From the Women in World Cultures Series; for their common features, see **260.**

The "overall theme of the book[s] is the diversity of women's lives in historic and contemporary Africa." Volume I touches on "the economic contributions that women have made, particularly as farmers and traders, and the political, military, and religious roles played by individual women or women's groups," as well as on "some family arrangements, including polygyny, woman-woman marriage, and brother/sister relationships"; on problems created by the different views Europeans had of women; and gives accounts of "some of the women who tried to fight unsuccessfully against European take-overs." Approximately one-third of Volume II focuses on South Africa; the rest "deals with the various ways in which African women helped their countries gain independence from colonialism, the diversity of life-styles in Africa and the current problems facing African women." Art and statistics are used as points of departure for thoughtful student exercises.

256. Hay, Margaret Jean, and Stichter, Sharon, eds. ***African Women South of the Sahara.*** New York: Longman, 1984. 225p. $13.95.

Eleven articles by scholars from the fields of history, anthropology, sociology, economics, political science, literature, and art history examine "the range of variations in women's social position in [sub-Saharan] Africa, taking into account not only the great diversity of traditional social arrangements, but also the overlay of outside influences, from European colonial conquest in the late nineteenth and early twentieth centuries to the Arab/Islamic penetration of earlier eras."

Topics covered include women in rural and urban economies, in politics and national liberation movements, religion and secular ideology, literature and the arts, and the changing family.

Clear, concise, crammed with digestibly presented information using both statistics and quotations from women's own statements, and setting forth thought-provoking conclusions that summarize and highlight the authors' arguments, this book set out to "incorporate and synthesize the best insights of the new scholarship in the field," and does so.

Intended for undergraduates and the general public, it is readable by able 12th graders. Valuable sixteen-page bibliography identifies items most useful to nonspecialists.

257. Mba, Nina Emma. ***Nigerian Women Mobilized: Women's Political Activity in Southern Nigeria, 1900–1965.*** Berkeley: University of California Institute of International Studies, 1982. 348p. $12.95.

Based largely on unpublished primary sources and personal interviews, this book focuses on the effects of historical change on the "motivations and self-images of the women and the objectives, organization, leadership, and effectiveness of their protest movements and political associations." It covers the position of women before 1900 and the effects of colonization, the women's war of 1929 and mass protest movements thereafter, and the transition from traditional to modern politics. Selectively assignable to able 12th graders; 21-page bibliography.

258. Robertson, Claire C., and Klein, Martin A., eds. ***Women and Slavery in Africa.*** Madison: University of Wisconsin Press, 1983. 380p. $22.50.

Seventeen articles by specialists in the field present a combination of theoretical analysis and empirical research. Couched in palatable prose, illustrated by case histories, with excerpts from original sources and statistics, the articles are both informative and provocative. They explore questions about the productive and reproductive functions of slave women; women's roles as slave owners, overseers, dealers, and beneficiaries of slave labor; and the impact of colonization.

The area covered is sub-Saharan Africa; articles deal both with the Atlantic slave trade and the internal African trade. Most of the papers fall within the period from the early nineteenth to the early twentieth century. Some of the articles could be assigned to able 12th graders.

259. Strobel, Margaret. "African Women's History." ***The History Teacher*** 15, no. 4 (August 1982): 509–22.

Outlines both the difficulties and the opportunities in the study of African women's history. The problems are scant sources and the overall underdevelopment of social history in the African context; fruitful possibilities that could be explored are women's work, women's associations, legal status, and the impact on women of the state and of development. The author suggests supplementing history with fiction and social science data. Gives some information on subject matter, and sketches the major themes commonly treated, with reference to sources. Helpful as a guide to a very new field.

ASIAN HISTORY

260. Bingham, Marjorie Wall, and Gross, Susan Hill. ***Women in India: Vedic to Modern Times.*** Hudson, Wis.: Gary E. McCuen, 1980. 110p. $6.95.

Part of the Women in World Cultures Series, designed for and field-tested by high school students and meant to "supplement regular course offerings." The series weds careful scholarship to attention to the needs of pre-college students and their teachers, resulting in high-interest volumes with substantial content in palatable and eye-appealing form. Sensitive to issues of class and ethnicity, the volumes in this series combine contributions of notable women with information about life cycles, roles, legal and social status, and a regard for chronology. Use of quotations (a paragraph to a page or two from primary sources, in the women's own words whenever possible), government reports, anthropological data, and folklore is extensive. The ample illustrations are unusually well chosen, striking, and will promote discussion, though they are of varying technical quality. "Points to Consider," addressed to students following the sections within each volume, are generally thought provoking while rooted in the text. With some help, the series is accessible to slower 9th grade readers, but it is most appropriate with average 10th graders; able 11th and 12th graders may find it too elementary. Each unit offers a glossary, a bibliography, and maps when needed. The rather pedestrian *Teacher's Guide* (20p., $1.25) include some historical background, concepts to be covered, objectives for each chapter, and answers to the "Points to Consider." Filmstrips for the series ($29.95) tend to be technically competent but unexciting, and rely heavily on portraits.

The focus of *Women in India* is "the overriding factor affecting Indian women since medieval times . . . the cultural emphasis on marriage." The curriculum starts by considering "a shift in attitude towards women" from the Vedas to Manu, and goes on to deal with "complexities of Hindu marriage," especially as affected by the caste system; "woman's loss of status and its effects," including child marriage, *sati,* infanticide, and purdah; "diversity of roles," with sections on tribal women, *devadasi,* and caste differences; nineteenth- and twentieth-century reform, involving *sati,* widow remarriage, and education; and the contemporary status of women, including an analysis of ten "women leaders in India." The authors note that they "do not deal directly with two critical aspects of Hindu Indian society that have also affected women: the joint family and the problem of population control."

261. Bingham, Marjorie Wall, and Gross, Susan Hill. ***Women in Traditional China: Ancient Times to Modern Reform.*** 120p. $6.95. ***Women in Modern China: Transition, Revolution and Contemporary Times.*** 106p. $6.95. Hudson, Wis.: Gary E. McCuen, 1980. From the Women in World Cultures Series; for their common features see **260.**

These volumes take admirable care to distinguish between evidence and interpretation in coverage of "The Very Distant Past," and combine successfully the simultaneous teaching of content, concepts, and method, as in "Women and Education in China: An Activity to Interpret Sources." Information on footbinding, concubinage, women warriors, the stages of the life cycle, and diversity (the Manchu, Mongols, and the Norsu; slave women and women slave owners) is given. Guomindang and Communist attitudes toward women, peasant women, village change, and political leaders is discussed. There are also individual chronological sections.

262. Chipp, Sylvia A., and Green, Justin J., eds. ***Asian Women in Transition.*** University Park: Pennsylvania State University Press, 1980. 256p. $12.50.

Eleven articles (seven of them by political scientists) explore the links between women's status and access to important economic activity, inheritance patterns, kinship systems, and the dominant religion in China, Japan, the Philippines, Indonesia, Malaysia, India, Pakistan, and Bangladesh. Most give a historical background before concentrating on contemporary changes. Based on field research, they also address some (largely social science-derived) theoretical issues, and provide a good, if at times somewhat technical and narrowly focused, overview of a complex field.

263. Crown, Bonnie R. "Women's Lives in the Asian Tradition." ***Social Education*** 43, no. 4 (April 1979): 248–57.

This is a short discussion of traditional literature, with emphasis on women's feelings expressed in their own words. Included are over a dozen brief (a stanza to a page in length) selections from poems, letters, and diaries from Japan, Java, China, and Viet Nam. The author makes suggestions for student analysis and further reading for both teachers and students. Immediately useful in a variety of contexts with 9th to 12th grade students.

ISLAMIC AND MIDDLE EASTERN HISTORY

264. Bingham, Marjorie Wall, and Gross, Susan Hill. ***Women in Islam: The Ancient Middle East to Modern Times.*** Hudson, Wis.: Gary E. McCuen, 1980. 129p. $6.95. From the Women in World Cultures Series; for their common features see **260.**

This volume contrasts women's roles in economic, religious, and political spheres in ancient civilizations, where "female gods were worshipped, . . . queens did reign and . . . women made open contributions" to economic life, with "later, more patriarchal societies that tended to seclude and restrict women." In loosely chronological sequence, units deal with influential individual women; polygynous marriage; property rights; relationships with family and friends; the diversity of roles among different groups, from cloistered harem women to the Tuaregs with their considerable freedom; and women in nationalistic wars and revolutions, from Algiers to Iran and Egypt.

265. Bingham, Marjorie Wall, and Gross, Susan Hill. ***Women in Israel: Biblical Times to the Present.*** Hudson, Wis.: Gary E. McCuen, 1980. 87p. $6.95. From the Women in World Cultures Series; for their common features see **260.**

Starting with an analysis of women's images in the Bible, this book covers the "plow women" immigrants before World War I; the suffrage issue; the role of women in the military, historically and now; women in politics and the arts; kibbutz, Bedouin, and Arab women; and the current overall status of women in Israel.

266. Fernea, Elizabeth Warnock, and Bezirgan, Basima Quattan, eds. ***Middle Eastern Muslim Women Speak.*** Austin: University of Texas Press, 1977. 452p. $12.50.

Twenty-three selections on a wide variety of topics by contributors from the Muslim world—Morocco, Afghanistan, Egypt, Turkey, etc.—span the period from 600 A.D. to the present. There are excerpts from the Koran, from autobiographies, letters, fiction, and interviews, as well as lullabies, poems, and songs. The authors are mystics, writers, reformers, revolutionaries; they come from tribal, rural, urban, and a variety of family backgrounds and classes. Selections of a dozen or so pages give a good sense of what life is like for a Bedouin, a rural Moroccan, and an urban working-class Lebanese woman; these could usefully be compared by students. An introduction provides some historical, social, and religious context; headnotes of a page or so give biographical details; occasional notes explain the unfamiliar. The forty-three photographs help give a feel for the setting and the people. Level of reading difficulty varies; some selections would be suitable for competent 10th grade readers and up.

267. Hussain, Freda, ed. ***Muslim Women.*** New York: St. Martin's Press, 1984. 240p. $22.50.

Ten articles by "historians, sociologists, educationalists, political scientists, social anthropologists and an expert in French Maghrebian literature" discuss Muslim women in the Sudan, Tunisia, Egypt, Turkey, Iran, Pakistan, and Malaysia. Sensitive to the differences between cultural ideals and the realities of women's lives, and historically oriented, contributors explore Islamic prescriptions; the images of women in literature; early feminist movements; and legal, educational, and economic factors relevant to changes in women's roles. Scholarly but readable by the nonspecialist, the text is illustrated by statistics and excerpts from original sources.

268. Waddy, Charis. ***Women in Muslim History.*** New York: Longman, 1980. 224p. $27.95.

A descriptive rather than analytical work, this book sets out to "sketch the portraits of a few of the many women who take the stage, and outline certain of the scenes in which they play their part." The narrative ranges from the time of Muhammad and the caliphs through medieval Baghdad, Sicily, Cairo, and Spain, the Mongol Timurid and Ottoman Turkish periods, and twentieth-century Egypt, Pakistan, and other Muslim areas. The biographically oriented approach features primarily "notable" women, and relies heavily on literary sources. It is informative, and readable by competent 11th graders; for teachers intending to use it, however, some previous theoretical knowledge of women's history is advisable.

LATIN AMERICAN HISTORY

269. Arrom, Silvia Marina. "Teaching the History of Hispanic-American Women." ***The History Teacher*** 13, no. 4 (August 1980): 493–507.

Discusses approaches to the subject based on the syllabus provided, which outlines topics and lists readings and films, a number of which are discussed in the text. Considered are *marianismo,* the cult of feminine spiritual superiority, which is the complement of machismo; the recognized public importance of women's family activities; the importance of class and race; and the impact of the Church. Although many of the suggested readings are very specialized, some can be useful even at the high school level.

270. Lavrin, Asuncion. "Women in Latin American History." ***The History Teacher*** 14, no. 3 (May 1981): 387–99.

Suggests topics for study and presents a chronologically arranged bibliography, without annotations, but with subheadings such as "the uncommon and the common woman," "black women," "Indian women," "marriage and the family," "travellers' impressions," and "work, education and feminism." Also lists books "with illustrations appropriate for slides."

271. Martin, Luis. ***Daughters of the Conquistadores: Women of the Viceroyalty of Peru.*** Albuquerque: University of New Mexico Press, 1983. 416p. $14.95.

Written with "the student of history in mind," and ranging over the three centuries following the conquest, this book examines "the role played by women, . . . the system of female education, the colonial marriages, the daily life of women in the colonial cities, and their impact on the colonial church." The author feels that "the three cultural forces of Don Juanism, marianism, and courtly love played a dominant role in shaping their self-awareness and behavior." Numerous vivid, detailed case studies illustrate generalizations based on an extensive study of manuscript and early printed sources. The story is very largely that of the social and economic elite, and makes "no attempt to study black or Indian women." Some of the occasional references are jarring, as that to concubines who were "frequently a sensuous mulatta or mestiza, occasionally an exotic morisca." Tending to the anecdotal, the individual vignettes that make up the bulk of the text do add up to a good feel for the flavor of life for women in colonial Peru. A selection of the brief biographical sketches and stories could be assigned to competent 11th grade students and up. Includes an eleven-page research-oriented bibliography.

272. Navarro, Marysa. "Review Essay: Research on Latin American Women." ***Signs*** 5, no. 1 (Autumn 1979): 111–20.

Gives a general overview and examples of recent work by authors whose main objective is understanding "how the capitalist mode of production in its dependent form" operates, and situating women in this context. Both substantive and theoretical contributions are discussed.

MATHEMATICS

273. Fox, Lynn H. ***The Problem of Women and Mathematics.*** New York: Ford Foundation, 1981. 40p. Free.

A summary of the research literature, this booklet deals with the nature and extent of sex differences in learning, study, and aptitude for mathematics. It examines the factors influencing the study, learning, and career choice of mathematics, and the extent to which sex differences in mathematics learning, study, or aptitude are related to different career outcomes for women and men. Approximately one-third of the book deals with possibilities of, suggestions for, and descriptions of programs that have sought to effect an increase in women's participation and success in mathematics. Crammed with information, lucid, and readable, this is a good introduction to the issues and to what is being done for women in this area.

274. Fox, Lynn H.; Fennema, Elizabeth; and Sherman, Julia, eds. ***Women and Mathematics: Research Perspectives for Change.*** Washington, D.C.: National Institute of Education, 1977. 206p. $16.15. Available from ERIC, 3900 Wheeler Avenue, Alexandria, Va. 22304. Request document # ED 160403.

The three papers in this volume: "The Effects of Sex Role Socialization on Mathematics Participation and Achievement," "Influences of Selected Cognitive, Affective, and Educational Variables on Sex-Related Differences in Mathematics Learning and Studying," and "Effects of Biological Factors on Sex-Related Differences in Mathematics Achievement," were an outgrowth of the authors' own research and of their investigation of the literature current at the time of writing. Each includes an analytical review of the available research and an extensive bibliography. The papers show that sex differences in mathematical achievement "do not appear to be linked to biological differences"; that they are "largely a function of differential course taking"; that they are related to girls not seeing "the usefulness of mathematics to their future roles"; and that "characteristics of teachers, instruction and school organization" affect women's participation and achievement in mathematics. Easy to grasp arguments and clear organization of data make for a good introduction to the issues, to authoritative information, and to possibilities for corrective action.

275. Kaseberg, Alice; Kreinberg, Nancy; and Downie, Diane. ***Equals***. Berkeley, Calif.: Lawrence Hall of Science, 1980. 134p. $5.00.

This is primarily a handbook for organizing inservice workshops for educators. Consisting of projects, games, research questions, teaching strategies, and activities that emphasize the importance of mathematics in employment and stimulate problem-solving skills, much of this is directly applicable in high school classrooms. Includes an annotated resource list.

276. Perl, Teri. ***Math Equals: Biographies of Women Mathematicians + Related Activities***. Reading, Mass.: Addison-Wesley, 1978. 250p. $11.95.

An unusual interdisciplinary combination of biography, history, and hands-on mathematics, this imaginative book has verve and intellectual integrity. It presents engaging and readable accounts of the historical context, lives, and work of nine women "who have made significant contributions to mathematics," from Hypatia in the fifth century, to du Châtelet in the eighteenth, Somerville in the nineteenth, and Noether in the twentieth. Enriched with apt and thought-provoking quotations by its subjects as well as some about them by their contemporaries, the accounts "raise questions about roles of women, and obstacles placed by family and society on the development of [their] talents." The mathematical activities relate to the fields in which the women discussed had worked. Though most of the activities deal with topics not usually introduced in early math courses (Venn and Chladni diagrams, function, rates of change and limit, finite differences, Euler's law) they are "accessible to anyone with elementary school mathematics and geometry," may be explored in any sequence, and are very well presented. The book as a whole is challenging but not difficult, and is certainly rewarding. Even less able students could handle it with some teacher support, 10th grade and up. The book has been field-tested for high school appeal.

277. Tobias, Sheila. ***Overcoming Math Anxiety.*** Boston: Houghton Mifflin, 1980. 288p. $7.95.

Summarizes research about the relationships among gender, mathematics, and spatial visualization; explains the nature and roots of math anxiety and avoidance; and suggests specific strategies, outlined in detail, that can be used in the classroom or individually to overcome both. Helpful also in pinpointing the difficulties that students experience in doing math, and showing how to help to overcome them. The listing of organizations, math workshops, and math therapy programs is out of date but useful in providing a starting place for inquiry after current ones. A teacher resource; exercises can be of immediate use in class.

278. Tobias, Sheila, and Weissbrod, Carol. "Anxiety and Mathematics: An Update." ***Harvard Educational Review*** 2 (February 1980): 63–70.

Includes extensive bibliography.

SCIENCE

279. Aldrich, Michele L. "Review Essay: Women in Science." ***Signs*** 4, no. 1 (Autumn 1978): 126–35.

Examines work on the following topics: statistics on women in science, women as students of science and in the history of science, conferences, and major studies on women in science.

280. Bleier, Ruth. ***Science and Gender: A Critique of Biology and Its Theories on Women.*** New York: Pergamon Press, 1984. 219p. $12.50.

A convenient interdisciplinary overview, the empirical data and references in this book are most solid in the purely biological areas. The author considers conditions under which biological determinism emerges as the explanation for social, political, and economic inequality; the theories of human cultural evolution; and sexuality, ideology, and patriarchy. She also critiques sociobiological theory; the studies linking hormones with aggression and intelligence; and brain lateralization with sex differences in cognitive abilities. She examines the work of feminist anthropologists, and discusses "a feminist science that begins by discarding dualistic assumptions as well as concepts of control and dominance and of linear causality."

281. Hubbard, Ruth; Henifin, Mary Sue; and Fried, Barbara, eds. ***Biological Woman—The Convenient Myth: A Collection of Feminist Essays and a Comprehensive Bibliography.*** Cambridge, Mass.: Schenkman, 1982. 376p. $11.95.

A collection of twelve articles with an introduction that discusses the need to be aware of the inescapable subjectivity involved in scientific investigation, and in scientists' choice of subjects to investigate and questions to ask. The articles critique the sexism of evolutionary theory and sociobiology; point out the sexist effects of language used in scientific discussions of biological sex differences and of right and left brain specialization; discuss the takeover from midwives by male physicians, sterilization abuse, and hormonal theories of lesbianism; provide notes for a course on black women's health; explore the interaction of culture and biology in the areas of muscular development, physical performance, height, and hormones; and relate the personal experiences of a woman scientist. This last, as well as the introduction, could usefully be read by 11th and 12th graders. Included are thirty worthwhile illustrations, from archival photographs to cartoons and advertisements. A 37-page bibliography on "women, science and health" is arranged under thirty-three headings, including evolution, sexualities, sex differences, addictions, birth control, eating, psychology, women in the Third World, science, biographies, and history.

282. Hubbard, Ruth, and Lowe, Marion, eds. ***Genes and Gender II: Pitfalls in Research on Sex and Gender.*** New York: Gordian Press, 1979. 154p. $6.95.

The authors state that "science is a product of the human imagination, created from theory-laden facts" and that "scientists' social perspectives and experiences inevitably cloud their sight and guide what they deem worthy of notice, as well as the meaning and validity of what they notice." The seven articles written in this context provide a feminist critique of sociobiology and of the theory of male dominance among primates, of sex differences in aggression and brain asymmetry, as well as examining transsexualism. Fare for those with particular interest in the topics covered. In volume I, some of the selections are sociological, and the biological ones are technical.

283. Kammer, Ann E.; Granrose, Cherlyn S.; and Sloan, Jan B. ***Science, Sex and Society.*** Newton, Mass.: Education Development Center, 1979. 569p. $15.75.

The authors' goals here are "to illustrate the web of interrelationships among science, people, and society; to demystify science; to illuminate the influence of science on women; . . . to examine the challenges facing a woman who wishes to be a scientist, wife and mother; and to encourage young women with talents to use those talents." Thirty-eight motley articles, not uniformly well chosen, include "The Anomaly of a Woman in Physics," "Mathematics and Sex," "Florence Rena Sabini," "The Natural Sciences," "Working Wives: a Racial Comparison," and "Can We Be Feminist Physicians?" Brief headnotes introduce each of several groups of articles;

each group is followed by a bibliography and a resource list. There are also six simple lab exercises that relate to work done by women scientists, about whom information is featured. The articles vary from lively personal accounts to statistics; narratives range from the prosaic to the humdrum. Many of the articles would be readable by competent and interested 11th and 12th graders.

284. Keller, Evelyn Fox. "Feminism and Science." ***Signs*** 7, no. 3 (Spring 1982): 589–602.

Insofar as objectivity is possible, this is an objective and balanced discussion of liberal and radical feminist criticism of science. Issues range from the lack of equal opportunity for women in science as a profession, to the charge of bias in the choice of problems to be researched and funded and in the design and interpretation of experiments, and in scientific language, to the rejection of objectivity itself as an ideology. Clear and concise, but not easy reading.

285. Keller, Evelyn Fox. ***Reflections on Gender and Science.*** New Haven: Yale University Press, 1985. 193p. $17.95.

Assuming that both gender and science are socially constructed categories, nine essays by a mathematical biophysicist ask: "How much of the nature of science is bound up with the idea of masculinity, and what would it mean for science if it were otherwise?" Using historical, psychological, and scientific/philosophical perspectives, Keller explores a wide range of issues including Plato's epistemology, Baconian science, cognitive repression in contemporary physics, and "the force of the pacemaker concept in theories of aggregation in cellular slime mold." The focus of her interest is the "interdependencies between subjectivity and objectivity, between feeling and reason." This is a thought-provoking, clearly argued, scholarly treatment of a difficult topic. The use of specific illustrative detail to support and illuminate theory helps to make it accessible to the nonspecialist.

286. Kohlstedt, Sally Gregory. "In from the Periphery: American Women in Science, 1830–1880." ***Signs*** 4, no. 1 (Autumn 1978): 81–96.

The narrative gives information about individual women and discusses the reactions of society and the scientific establishment to their work.

287. Rossiter, Margaret W. ***Women Scientists in America: Struggles and Strategies to 1940.*** Baltimore: Johns Hopkins University Press, 1982. 464p. $10.95.

"As scientists they were atypical women; as women they were unusual scientists." Seeking to "identify major and minor figures, to analyze significant education and employment patterns, to note striking achievements and to examine the types of recognition accorded (or withheld)," the author has produced a fascinating pioneer study. She documents the numerical rise of women scientists from "about ten at a few early women's colleges" in the late nineteenth century to the thousands in various fields and institutions by 1940—though "at the price of accepting a pattern of segregated employment and underrecognition." Topics discussed include women's access to scientific education; the rising expectation that "their training lead somewhere," and their entry into positions as assistants; the effects of the professionalization and hence "masculinizing" of science and of the women's movement; academic, government, and industrial employment; and double standards and "compensatory recognition." There is information on female presidents of national scientific societies, notable couples in science, unemployment and marriage rates, and publication. Scholarly writing in lucid and vigorous prose is interwoven with quotations from original sources. Included are thirty-five illustrations and twenty-nine tables. The seventeen-page bibliography is heavily research oriented. A stimulating teacher resource, this is the only study of its kind.

SOCIAL SCIENCE

ANTHROPOLOGY AND CROSS-CULTURAL STUDIES

288. Etienne, Mona, and Leacock, Eleanor, eds. ***Women and Colonization: Anthropological Perspectives.*** New York: Praeger, 1980. 352p. $14.95.

"Case studies of women's economic, social and political roles in 12 societies [7 Native American, 3 African, and 2 Pacific], and the changes that followed European colonization . . . [based on] missionary reports, explorers' and traders' accounts, and other historical records," and written from the perspective of those colonized. The introduction outlines the "ethnocentric, male-centered" and ahistorical approaches in anthropology that have been "an obstacle to the understanding of societies different from our own." The position of women (often more egalitarian than has been thought) cross-culturally at the time of the European conquest and under colonization, and women's resistance and resignation to colonization are also discussed. Each case study is preceded by a page-long historical headnote liberally studded with excerpts from primary sources, and followed by a list of references. Scholarly but readable by the nonspecialist.

289. Hunter, Lisa K., Project Director. ***Sources of Strength: Women and Culture.*** Newton, Mass.: Education Development Center, 1979. 702p. $15.95. 2 oral history interview tapes, $1.75 each.

An effectively presented cross-cultural study of women in African, Chinese, African-American, and Chinese-American societies. Not only an informative and sensitive examination of women's options and limitations in the personal, economic, and political spheres of each society, but helpful to students in relating the information presented to their own lives. A solid background in the history and culture of each society, imaginative teaching strategies, and suggested student learning materials are provided for teachers. For students, there are numerous short, easy-to-read, high-interest excerpts from sources that lean toward the literary. See **9** for the companion annotated bibliography. High school level.

290. Iglitzin, Lynne B., and Ross, Ruth, eds. ***Women in the World: A Comparative Study.*** Santa Barbara, Calif.: ABC-Clio, 1976. 427p. $11.75.

Twenty-four essays by political scientists, historians, and sociologists review the position of women in the economy, education, law, and politics in the following countries: Britain, France, West Germany, Ireland, Italy, the U.S.S.R., Yugoslavia, Algeria, Ghana, Iran, Israel, Columbia, Mexico, and China. There are also more general discussions of African, Latin American, and Muslim women. Each of four sections, on conceptualizing cross-cultural study, on women in Europe and the United States, on women in developing countries, and on women in "nations mobilized for social change," gives an overview of salient points. In addition to a lot of factual information, usually including a historical sketch, the authors are concerned with the " 'reality gap' between official government pronouncements and legislation . . . and the traditional behavior and attitudes of a large portion of the population." The not always positive relationship between modernization and female equality, the loss of women's power due to new values imposed by Western colonialism, and the ways in which Western research biases have distorted our views of realities in developing countries are also handled with sensitivity. The scholarly text, readable by nonspecialists, provides a good introduction to some complex and important subjects.

291. Lindsay, Beverly, ed. ***Comparative Perspectives of Third World Women: The Impact of Race, Sex, and Class.*** New York: Praeger, 1983. 334p. $14.95.

Twelve contributors, a number of them Third World women, write on women in developing countries: Africa in general; Zaire, Kenya, China, North India, the Caribbean, and Cuba; and on minority women in the United States: Native American, black, Chicana, and Vietnamese. The tone of the writing varies, since "some elected to work in an objective and scholarly genre, while others attempted to portray more humanistic and subjective views." The eighteen-page introduction discusses conceptual issues. Some of the articles are marred by abstruse and technical writing, which surrounds the concrete, interesting, and up-to-date information useable in the classroom.

292. Lorimer, T. ***Illustrative Statistics on Women in Selected Developing Countries.*** Washington, D.C.: Department of Commerce, 1980. Available from the U.S. Government Printing Office. 24p. $3.50.

Information on twenty-seven countries in Africa, Asia, and Latin America, including Ghana, Kenya, Morocco, Senegal, Tanzania, Bangladesh, Taiwan, India, Indonesia, Pakistan, Turkey, Brazil, Chile, Columbia, Guatemala, Jamaica, Mexico, and Peru is presented in thirteen charts. Topics cover women's age, urban/rural residence, and data on marriage, fertility, mortality, education, and occupation. Each chart is set up to make comparisons easy, and most invite comparisons with data on men. Useful adjunct to **255, 260.** For suggestions on classroom uses of statistics, see **196.**

293. Mead, Margaret. ***Sex and Temperament in Three Primitive Societies.*** New York: Morrow, 1963. 306p. $6.95.

Classic study done in New Guinea in 1933, showing that female and male sexual stereotypes vary in different societies. Mead suggests that the ideal for both sexes may be the same in one of the societies, approximating what we think of as "masculine"; in the second society, the ideal for both sexes may come closer to our stereotypical idea of "feminine"; in the third society, the ideal for men is similar to our "feminine" ideal, while for women, our "masculine" stereotype is the ideal. Remains useful, in spite of recent controversy surrounding the author. Sections may be assigned to competent 11th and 12th grade readers.

294. Rapp, Rayna. "Review Essay: Anthropology." ***Signs*** 4, no. 3 (Spring 1979): 497–513.

Discusses investigations of "the ambiguous nature of specific contexts of sexual subordination" in both historical and contemporary cultures, seen as a continuation of the debate about the "universality of sexual asymmetry."

295. Reiter, Rayna R., ed. ***Toward an Anthropology of Women.*** New York: Monthly Review Press, 1976. 416p. $7.50.

Seventeen essays "assume that women's experience may be different from that of men," and "subject our notions of male dominance to specific analysis." Writers discuss "dominance" among nonhuman primates; the "man the hunter" model of cultural evolution; early family forms and those among contemporary hunter/gatherers; the "matriarchy debate"; the egalitarian societies of Bushmen and Australian aborigines; and analyses of women's status among West European peasant groups, in China, and in several African and Latin American countries. Some of the approaches use Marxist-feminist theory; none are polemical; the style is generally nontechnical, jargon-free, and reasonably readable. The twenty-page bibliography leans toward the technical and specialized.

296. Smith, Robert J., and Wiswell, Ella Lury. ***The Women of Suye Mura.*** Chicago: University of Chicago Press, 1983. 320p. $7.50.

An anthropological study of "the daughters, sisters, wives, mothers and grandmothers of farm households, as well as those of small merchants and artisans" in a Japanese village less than forty years after the modernizing legislation of the Meiji era. Topics covered are the nature of women and their world, formal associations, interpersonal relations in and out of the family, sex, socialization, and "the handicapped, misfits, wanderers and witches." Useful as a supplement to textbook history. Also, because the book directly quotes the vigorous, vividly written field notes, which in turn quote the often pithy sayings of Suye women, it can be used to study the anthropologist's method and to give insight into the attitudes of her subjects. A comparison with the classic study, *Suye Mura: A Japanese Village,* by J. F. Embree, Wiswell's husband, sheds further light both on similarities and differences in approach by a male and a female observer, and on the life of the people in the village. Selectively readable by able 11th and 12th graders.

297. Valiant, Sharon. ***Crossing Cultures II: Third World Women.*** New Brunswick, N.J.: Consortium for Educational Equity, Rutgers University, 1983. 36p. $4.00.

In this "book of materials, activities and ideas for the classroom teacher," the focus is on Asian, Asian-American, black, Hispanic, and Native American women. Arranged under the headings "Myths and Legends," "Learning about Lives," "The Makers," and "Notable Women," it features brief annotated bibliographies grouped by geographical areas. Listed are biographies, novels, histories, conference reports, and some audiovisual resources, with appropriate grade level use indicated. Also featured are immediately useable, varied suggestions for classroom projects, reports, bulletin board displays, and discussions. High school level.

POLITICAL SCIENCE

298. Baxter, Sandra, and Lansing, Marjorie. ***Women and Politics: The Visible Majority.*** Rev. ed. Ann Arbor: University of Michigan Press, 1983. 259p. $10.95.

This book "explores changes in the political attitudes and behavior of women over the last 25 years," argues for the existence of a significant "voting bloc" among women and for the importance of women's impact on politics through voluntary organizations, and explores reasons for "the failure of women to win elections" and to hold "elite decision-making posts." Throughout, politics are linked to the broader culture, and comparative data is offered on Britain, France, West Germany, and Denmark to show how "different institutional and historical factors produce different levels of political participation by women." Explored are women's voting behavior, attitudes toward politics, views on public policy, candidates, political parties, and political participation, all with attention to differences in time, race, class, and place. There are two chapters on black women voters. Crammed with information.

299. Berkin, Carol R., and Lovett, Clara M., eds. ***Women, War and Revolution.*** New York: Holmes & Meier, 1980. 310p. $13.50.

In these eleven articles, specialists deal with the themes of "women's emerging political consciousness and increased visibility during revolutionary movements and wars and with the rising expectations that ensue among them," the tension between "patriarchal and egalitarian values" resulting from the impact of the heightened female expectations, and "the development in very different historical contexts of one particularly interesting mechanism for resolving that tension: the ideal of civic motherhood." Periods and countries dealt with include the American, French, Italian, Chinese, and Cuban revolutions, Nazi Germany, World Wars I and II, and communist feminism. Introductions to each of the thematic sections discuss the major issues raised by the articles therein. A good choice for those ready to progress beyond **229.** Includes eight pages of illustrations and a twelve-page annotated bibliography.

300. Carroll, Berenice A. "Review Essay: Political Science, Part I: American Politics and Political Behavior." ***Signs*** 5, no. 2 (Winter 1979): 289–306.

Provides substantive information as well as theoretical analysis. Discusses works covering topics such as men's predominance in public office holding, the "marginality" of women in the political process, and the lack of a major impact of feminist scholarship on the discipline.

301. Carroll, Berenice A. "Review Essay: Political Science, Part II: International Politics, Comparative Politics, and Feminist Radicals." ***Signs*** 5, no. 3 (Spring 1980): 449–58.

Touches on the absence of the theme of patriarchy as it applies to women in the literature of the discipline, and on the challenges posed by lesbian feminist and Marxist feminist writers.

302. Newland, Kathleen. ***Women in Politics: A Global Review.*** Washington, D.C.: Worldwatch Institute, 1975. 45p. $2.00.

Presents interesting data haphazardly on a variety of topics relevant to the subject: In 1975, only in nine countries, comprising under 0.5 percent of the world's female population, were women "by law excluded from political processes open to men"; in 1966, "the President of the Dominican Republic appointed women to the governorships of all 26 provinces." China has fixed women's share in offices of the Revolutionary Committees of the communes at 30 percent. The first four women members of the French Government were responsible for hospitals, children, prisons, and women. Although its most recent figures are for 1975, this pamphlet is still useful as a handy overview in a rather random and inconsistent selection of countries. There are at least some data for the major European powers, for a sprinkling of other European nations east and west, and for Third World countries, with some representation of each continent.

PSYCHOLOGY

303. Gappa, Judith M., and Pearce, Janice. ***Assessing the Introductory Psychology Course.*** Washington, D.C.: American Psychological Association, 1980. 81p. $7.50. American Psychological Association, 1200 17 Street, N.W., Washington, D.C. 20036.

Created for the busy teachers of introductory courses, this volume provides gender-related information that can be immediately used in areas commonly covered: the nature, fields, application, and history of psychology; research design, methodology, and statistics; psychological testing and measurement; biological, cognitive-affective, social, and individual bases of behavior; and psychological adjustment, with a number of subheadings under each. Provided are examples, discussion questions, and references to sources that give information with which to expand upon the suggestions made. Much of the book would be useful at the high school level. Includes an eight-page bibliography.

304. Frieze, Irene H.; Parsons, J. E.; Johnson, P. B.; Ruble, D. N.; and Zellman, G. L. ***Women and Sex Roles: A Social Psychological Perspective.*** New York: W. W. Norton, 1978. 444p. $12.95. *Instructor's Manual.* Free.

A basic text for college courses written from a feminist perspective. Encyclopedic, plain, and ponderous, it covers sexist bias in traditional psychology; psychoanalytic theories of Freud, Horney, Jung, and Erikson about the feminine personality; sex differences in intellectual abilities and personality; the bearing on the origins of sex differences of infant, anthropological, genetic, and hormonal studies, and of sex-role socialization theories; roles of women, both traditional and changing; role conflict; issues of achievement, discrimination, nonverbal dominance, politics, and power; and making life decisions. Includes a forty-two page list of references.

305. Maccoby, Eleanor Emmons, and Jacklin, Carol Nagy. ***The Psychology of Sex Differences.*** Vol. I: text. 391p. $8.95. Vol. II: annotated bibliography. 232p. $6.95. Stanford: Stanford University Press, 1974.

An examination of a vast body of research evidence from the journal literature concerning how the sexes do and don't differ in "intellectual performance, and social behaviors that are not specifically sexual but have been thought to be differentiated by sex." The "bulk of the work covered was done with white, middle class children and adults" from birth to college age. The authors identify themselves as feminists who "have tried to be objective about the value-laden topics discussed." In fact, their presentation is a model of the very best kind of scholarship: A vast body of serviceably organized material is commented on with trenchant insight, scrupulous fairness, and keen intelligence. Some of the topics covered are perception, learning, and memory; intellectual abilities; achievement motivation; activity level and emotionality; dominance; and theories on the origins of the differences. The only "fairly well established" sex differences found are: the greater verbal ability of females and the greater visual-spatial and mathematical ability and aggressiveness of males. Eighty-six evidence-summarizing tables are a great convenience. It takes a true devotee to read this cover to cover, but it remains a classic, and the single best authoritative reference source, in spite of its date, on all questions of putative intellectual and emotional sex differences. The bibliography lists contents of over 1,400 articles, three-quarters of them from between 1966 and 1974. The bibliographic "annotations" are actually summaries, in a format that gives the number and age of subjects, a detailed description of the method, and the results of each study included, serving as an acceptable substitute for reading the original.

306. Parlee, Mary Brown. "Review Essay: Psychology and Women." ***Signs*** 5, no. 1 (Autumn 1979): 121–33.

Surveys critiques of traditional psychological research on women, new empirical research from a feminist perspective, theoretical contributions, and the problems raised by psychology's commitment to the experimental method.

307. Rohrbaugh, Joanna Bunker. ***Women: Psychology's Puzzle.*** New York: Basic Books, 1981. 505p. $9.95.

Surveys a large body of new research, carefully separating opinion from evidence, and summarizing "the major themes and studies that relate to five key areas of female psychology and gender differences: biology, personality, social roles, bodily functions and mental health." After examining the formal theories and the research studies, these are compared with "women's own opinions and experiences." Topics covered include the role of hormones in behavior, intelligence, and emotions; a critique of the major theories of female personality development; sex-role stereotypes; psychological issues in marriage, motherhood, single living, and membership in minority groups; sexuality, contraception, abortion, pregnancy, childbirth, and rape; women's health issues, physical and mental; and domestic violence. The lean, vigorous, and graphic prose, studded with quotations from biologists, psychologists, sociologists, and feminists, proves that scholarship need not be either dull or jargon-ridden. A formidable volume of information; for all its readability, it will most likely be used as a reference source. The twenty-two-page bibliography is comprehensive and largely technical. There is considerable overlap in subject matter with **308,** but the latter has a sociological rather than a psychological perspective; it has a more markedly feminist, theoretical, and institutional orientation; is more densely argued; presents more, and more up-to-date (1980 census) statistics; and is less concerned with individual feelings and experience.

SOCIOLOGY

308. Andersen, Margaret L. ***Thinking about Women: Sociological and Feminist Perspectives.*** New York: Macmillan, 1983. 334p.

Wishing both to explain and to influence women's experience in society, the author feels that "sound feminist scholarship must entail an understanding of race, class and heterosexual relations." Referring often to the relevant historical background, the book starts with an examination of the feminist critique of sociology and goes on to discuss, among other topics, "biological sex and sociological gender," "sexism, science and society," sex-role socialization (including a useful section on formal schooling), women's work (with useful statistics from the 1980 census, and including "the political economy of housework"), "portraits of contemporary households," gender roles in the family, racism, the politics of reproduction, sexism and the social construction of knowledge, and crime and deviance. Separate chapters are devoted to liberal and radical feminism. Requires concentration to read and absorb, but is rewarding. The text is crowded with references to the twenty-nine-page bibliography, which draws heavily on recent research yet avoids being too technical.

309. Gappa, Judith M., and Pearce, Janice. ***Sex and Gender in the Social Sciences: Reassessing the Introductory Course.*** Includes "Guidelines for Introductory Sociology" and "Guidelines for Student-Faculty Communication." Washington, D.C.: American Sociological Association, 1982. 176p. $10.00 plus postage.

This guide, similar to **303,** provides a topical outline with detailed subheadings of areas commonly covered in introductory sociology courses: sociological theory, culture, norms, values, symbols, social stratification, groups, roles, etc. For each area, the authors give specific, concise suggestions about relevant sex- and gender-related content, and refer to those items in the nine-page bibliography (unfortunately not annotated) that document and expand on the suggestions. Also included are specific examples and discussion questions to use with students. Much of the book would be immediately useable in high school courses; it might be well to check some of the references.

310. Gould, Meredith. "Review Essay: The New Sociology." ***Signs*** 5, no. 3 (Spring 1980): 459–67.

Concentrates on emerging theoretical and methodological issues such as debate over "sex roles," critiques of androcentrism in sociological theory, interest in the sociology of knowledge, with some comment on the substantive implications of empirical research.

AUDIOVISUAL RESOURCES

INTERDISCIPLINARY APPROACHES

WOMEN'S STUDIES, WOMEN'S MOVEMENT, AND WOMEN'S RIGHTS

311. ***The American Woman: What Price Equality?*** Filmstrip, color. Cassette. *Guide*. 1980. $33.00. Social Studies School Service.

This updated program on women's rights deals with the right to vote in 1919 and job protection in 1964. It touches as well on remaining problems, from strong patriarchal social values to the criticism that women now have equality and freedom and must take advantage of it, that feminism reflects white middle-class rather than poor or minority women's concerns, and that many are satisfied with traditional roles.

312. ***"But the Women Rose": Voices of Women in American History.*** 2 records. Folkways FD 5535–6. $6.95 each. Ladyslipper.

Vol. I: Words of Anthony, Stowe, Truth, Stanton, Stone, Fuller, and others, narrated by five readers. Vol. II: Words of Jones, Goldman, Sanger, Friedan, Redstockings, Chisholm, and others, narrated by five readers.

313. ***How We Got the Vote (The American Documents Series).*** 53 mins. 16 mm. film, color. Order #70093. $22.00. University of Illinois.

Features popular songs lampooning women's rights, and voices of pioneers in the movement, including Alice Paul, who helped found the National Women's Party in 1916.

314. ***The New American Woman: 1848–1920.*** Filmstrip, color. Cassette/record. *Program Guide*. $35.00. Prentice-Hall Media.

The women's rights movement is traced from Seneca Falls through political action groups such as the Women's Christian Temperance Union.

315. ***Postcards.*** Several hundred postcards, available individually (4 × 6″ for 40¢ each/5 × 7″ for 50¢ each) or in any of twenty-seven topically grouped sets. Helaine Victoria Press.

The topics covered include Artists, Art Reproductions (almost all in full color, some of the other topics are in black and white or sepia), Authors, Aviation, Black and Afro Americans, Dance, Feminist Movement, Labor and Immigration, Music, Entertainment and Theater Arts, Native Americans, Science, Social Commentary, Suffrage, and Women/Language/Words. The nineteen-page catalog (50¢) reproduces miniatures of all the offerings, and provides detailed descriptions as well as some substantive information about the topics themselves.

316. ***Side by Side: Reenactments of Scenes from Women's History, 1848–1920.*** 2 record set. Galaxia 002. $11.95. Ladyslipper.

The words of women in the early struggle for women's rights in the United States, plus narration establishing the historical context.

317. ***Songs of the Suffragettes.*** Record. Folkways 5281. $8.95. Ladyslipper.

Sixteen authentic songs of the suffrage movement, with guitar and piano accompaniment.

318. ***A Woman's Place: The Women's Movement.*** Filmstrip, color. Cassette. *Program Guide*. 1974. $33.00. Prentice-Hall Media.

Charts the rise of the National Organization for Women, and of more radical women's groups; explores the dynamics of consciousness-raising groups and the formation of specialized action groups. Award winner.

319. ***The Women Get the Vote.*** 27 mins. 16mm. film, black and white. Rental $22.00. McGraw-Hill Films.

Using historic footage, this film covers the campaign for social, civil, and religious rights for women from 1848 to 1919.

320. ***The Women's Movement: Suffrage and Beyond.*** Three filmstrip/cassette programs. $60.00. Opportunities for Learning.

"The Cult of True Womanhood." 2 filmstrips. 40 frames, 11 mins. each. 2 cassettes/records. *Manual.* The evolution of this concept since 1800, its demise, and lingering aftereffects. Includes illustrations from contemporary magazines.

"Feminism as a Radical Movement." 2 filmstrips. Cassette. Struggle for the vote, and the disillusionment that followed.

"Is Anatomy Destiny?" A do-it-yourself audiovisual kit that offers the necessary background for a study of women's roles, problems, and opportunities.

321. ***Women's Rights in the U.S.: An Informal History.*** 27 mins. 16 mm. film, color. *Guide*. 1974. Order #82810. Rental $15.00. University of Illinois.

A dialogue between feminists and non-feminists from Abigail Adams to the present, based on speeches, diaries, and newspaper reports of famous and less well-known men and women, provides the commentary to a pictorial montage from sources of the period. Highlighted are the frontier, abolitionism, the Civil War, industrialization, and suffragism. Attitudes toward marriage, employment, fashion, and education are examined with wry humor. Award winner.

322. ***Women's Rights: Multicultural Equity.*** 4 cassettes with discussion questions. 1976. $22.00. National Education Association.

Comments by Patricia Ann Brown, Louise Jones, Mae T. Kim, Billie Nave Masters, and Consuelo Nieto.

MINORITY WOMEN

323. ***Beauty in the Bricks.*** 29 mins. 16 mm. film/videocassette, color. Rental $45.00. New Day Films.

Captures the positive side of life in a low-income housing project by following four energetic and creative black teenage girls as they braid hair, meet at the Girls' Club, flirt, gossip, and talk about their dreams. It shows that violence is a real part of their environment with the shooting of one of the girls' brother at a dance, and the casual conversations about rape and killings at a slumber party. But they strive, and at the close one of them is accepted to a high school for gifted students. Award winner.

324. ***Black Women's Speeches.*** 2 records. Vol. I, $8.95. Vol. II., $7.95. Ladyslipper.

Vol. I: Sojourner Truth, Sarah Parker Remond, Maria Stewart, Mary Church Terrell. Vol. II: Shirley Chisholm, Coretta Scott King, Angela Davis, Fannie Lee Chaney.

325. ***The Disabled Women's Theater Project.*** 60 mins. Videocassette, color. 1982. Rental $55.00. Women Make Movies.

Challenges the social attitudes perpetuating stereotypes about disabled women as undesirable in traditional female roles and as passive, dependent people. In a dynamic series of skits that deals with everything from the Avon salesperson to employment, public transportation, telethons, and kitchen chaos, the company conveys the absurd, funny, outrageous, painful, and dramatic moments of disabled women's lives.

326. ***Earth Mother: Voices of Native American Women.*** Filmstrip. Cassette. $25.00. Multi-Media Productions.

327. ***Klagetoh Maiden Singers.*** Record. Indian House 1508. $9.95. Ladyslipper.

Five Navajo women sing round, walking, and spin dances, and two-step songs.

328. ***Minority Youth: Angie.*** 10 mins. Film, color. Rental $32.00. BFA Educational Media.

Angie relates her personal feelings about being Mexican-American. She takes pride in the fact that Mexican-American families, like her family, "surround their kids with love instead of material things." But she questions the prejudice that she sees exhibited against Mexican-Americans, especially in education and employment opportunities.

329. ***Mitsuye and Nellie: Asian American Poets.*** 58 mins. 16 mm. film, color. Rental $75.00. Light-Saraf Films.

The poetry, ideas, and memories of a Japanese- and a Chinese-American woman are juxtaposed with rare newsreels and photos of seldom glimpsed areas of United States history. It is a film "about tenderness and anger between mothers and daughters, generational conflicts, and the breaking of stereotyped images of Asian American women"; it also "expresses, with dramatic clarity, the immigrant experience."

330. ***Our Songs Will Never Die.*** 35 mins. Film. Rental $48.00. Shenandoah Film Productions.

Yurok, Karuk, and Toluwa cultural summer camps are established to reconstruct early Native American village dance sites.

Young people work with tribal elders, and experience surf-fishing, sand-breadmaking, Indian card games, net making, and the history of their ancestors.

331. ***Pink Triangles.*** 35 mins. 16mm. film, color. 1983. Rental $50.00. *Study Guide,* $4.00. Cambridge Documentary Films.

Designed to explore prejudice against lesbians and gay men, to show some of the roots of prejudice and its current manifestations, this documentary discusses why the prejudice is so strong and makes connections with other forms of oppression: of women, blacks, radicals, and Jews. Features interviews with mental health workers, high school students, the parent of a lesbian, lesbians of various races, and gay men. It also provides a historical perspective, from the Middle Ages through the Nazi persecution and the McCarthy period in the United States. Arousal of deep personal feelings in viewers is an inevitable result of the screening of this film. The *Study Guide* advises how to provide the requisite structured and supportive environment for viewing, and gives detailed suggestions on how to handle resistance, confusion, hostility, and anxiety in the audience and in the discussion leader, as well as factual information on topics such as roles, parenting, medical and mental health, and aging among gay men and lesbians. The suitability of the film for high school students would have to be judged according to individual circumstances.

332. ***Roots to Cherish.*** 30 mins. Film. Rental $48.00. Shenandoah Film Productions.

A new film on American Indian pupils for those seeking to improve services to them in schools. Illustrates consequences of cultural differences on school performance, shows ways to conduct more appropriate evaluations, and suggests program modifications to improve individual pupil achievement.

333. ***Ruth Rubin: Yiddish Folk Songs.*** Record. Folkways 8720. $8.95. Ladyslipper.

Mostly Eastern European folksongs, sung unaccompanied. Includes one song by a Jewish child orphaned during World War II. *Booklet* has lyrics and information on Jewish history.

334. ***Suni Paz: Entre Hermanas (Between Sisters).*** Record. Folkways 8768. $8.95. Ladyslipper.

All the songs "support the strength and struggles of women." Chicana perspective. Comes with translation and notes.

335. ***Through Young People's Eyes.*** 29 mins. 16 mm. film/videocassette, color. Rental $50.00. The Cinema Guild.

Documentary portrait of black and Hispanic teenagers, mostly girls, growing up in a poor urban neighborhood. Interspersed with scenes of their everyday activities are interviews in which they candidly discuss the pleasures and pains of growing up. It shows teenagers in a positive light, allowing them to articulate their concerns about teachers and parents, boyfriends and marriage, school and parties, peer pressure and life goals.

WOMEN AND WORK

336. ***Always in Fashion.*** 20 mins. 16 mm. film, color. 1979. Order # 56472. Rental $12.50. University of Illinois.

Looks behind the scenes of the garment industry, where the hours are long, working conditions rotten, sweatshops abound, and women are exploited. Interviews with workers, manufacturers, contractors, and government officials explore the reasons why such conditions are tolerated.

337. ***Bread and Raises.*** Record/cassette. $8.00. Collector Records.

Thirteen songs span two hundred years of the struggles of working women to win equality and fair treatment in the workplace. Includes "Union Maid," "Fifty-nine Cents," "Solidarity Forever," "Bread and Roses," "Mother Jones," "I Am a Union Woman." The musical backup is in a mix of folk and country music styles.

338. ***Good Work, Sister!*** 20 mins. Videocassette/slides and cassette, color. Rental $30.00/$40.00. The Media Project.

Tells the stories of women who worked in the shipyards of Washington and Oregon from 1942 to 1945.

339. ***Hey Doc.*** 25 mins. 16 mm. film/videocassette. $425.00. Ask about rental. Carousel Films.

A documentary about a black physician who is medical advisor, confessor, and friend to the people of North Philadelphia's ghetto. The camera follows her to the schools, through slum streets, and into the lives of the addicted, the aged, and the angry.

340. ***Household Technicians.*** 28 mins. 16 mm. film/videocassette, color. 1976. English and Spanish versions on videocassette. Rental $50.00/$35.00 per day. Free preview. Martha Stuart Communications.

The women on this program are members of the fifth largest industry for women in the United States, employing 1.5 million, of whom over half are black. They discuss their work and their feelings, and how, through the National Committee on Household Employment, they are organizing to win the basic benefits and rights enjoyed by most American workers. Award winner from the series "Are You Listening?"

341. ***The Life and Times of Rosie the Riveter.*** 60 mins. 16 mm. film, color. Rental $85.00. Clarity Educational Productions.

Five former "Rosies," black and white, movingly recall their experiences as workers during the war in this award-winning film. Their testimony is interwoven with rare archival recruitment films, photographs, posters, advertisements, and music from the period. "An unusually tough-minded and intelligent documentary."—J. Hoberman, *Village Voice*. The *Teacher's Guide* (104p., $7.95) features sixty photographs, oral accounts, lively essays, biographical information about the women, and solid historical background, as well as discussion questions and projects.

342. ***No Handouts for Mrs. Hedgepeth.*** 27 mins. 16 mm. film, color. Order #11119. Rental $69.00. BFA Educational Media.

Mrs. Hedgepeth is a black domestic worker, among the millions of Americans who work hard and yet live at poverty level. She talks about her needs, frustrations, hopes, and disappointments; the film shows how her life contrasts with that of her middle-income employer.

343. ***On a Par, Not a Pedestal: Women in the Corporation.*** 26 mins. 16 mm. film, color. 1977. Order #84297. Rental $14.00. University of Illinois.

The film documents events at the Connecticut General Life Insurance Company, when women employees asked for and got a meeting with management to present their employment grievances. The resulting workshops, attended by over 4,000 people from all levels in the company, were filmed. The film captures the sense of an opening up among the men and women, and a shift away from the stereotyped attitudes toward the role of women in the organization.

344. ***Union Maids.*** 48 mins. 16 mm. film, black and white. Rental $70.00. New Day Films.

In this highly praised, multiple-award-winning film, three women share their experiences of the 1930s and the birth of the Congress of Industrial Organizations. They recall bad working conditions, the second-class treatment of women, their first union meetings, sit-down strikes, and facing police shotguns. Rare historical film footage and labor music of the period. *Study Guide* and *History Booklets* are also available.

345. ***The Willmar 8.*** 50 mins. 16 mm. film. 1980. Rental $75.00. California Newsreel.

Multiple-award-winning documentary story of eight unassuming, apolitical Midwestern women who were driven by sex discrimination in the workplace to start the longest bank strike in American history. They risked "jobs, friends, family and the opposition of Church and community . . . in a dramatic attempt to assert their own equality and self-worth."

346. ***With Babies and Banners: Story of the Women's Emergency Brigade.*** 45 mins. 16 mm. film, color. Rental $60.00. New Day Films.

Already a classic, this award-winning documentary shows the story of the women behind the successful strike against General Motors in Flint, Michigan in 1937, and makes connections between working women's issues then and now. Interviews with nine women of the Brigade are interwoven with excellent archival footage and photographs. Especially developed for high school use is a high quality curriculum packet, including a twenty-eight-page illustrated *Historical Booklet,* a fifteen-page *Student Activity Booklet* and a four-page *Teacher's Guide*.

347. ***Woman's Worth,*** by Janet Ridgeway (52p., $3.50, free with **345**), is an experiential teaching aid that provides background information, discussion questions, audits, surveys, and activities, many of which would be applicable to the high school classroom. Topics covered are the meaning of work, history of women in the workforce, occupational segregation, sex-role socialization, women and unions, comparable worth, and the role of church membership in the lives of activist women.

348. ***Women at Work: Choice and Challenge.*** 2 filmstrips. 2 cassettes/records. *Manual.* 1975. $79.50. The Center for Humanities.

Documentary of work-roles among poor, middle-class, and privileged women, from colonial times to the present. Includes interviews with an attorney, a mechanic, a medical technologist, and a secretary, and suggests new approaches to filling both work and family roles.

349. ***The Workplace Hustle.*** 30 mins. 16 mm. film, color. 1980. Order #90370. Rental $18.50. University of Illinois.

Studies male and female attitudes toward sexual harassment at work, defines sexual harassment, and gives statistics on its incidence.

ART

350. ***They Are Their Own Gifts—A Trilogy.*** Three 18 min. segments. 16 mm. film/videocassette, color. Rental $35.00 each/$80.00 for trilogy. New Day Films.

Award-winning documentary traces the lives of Muriel Rukeyser (poet), Alice Neel (painter), and Anna Sokolow (choreographer). "Activists as well as artists, their work comments on the social and political events of this century. The effect of the Depression and World War II on their childhoods, together with racial struggles and the Vietnam War on their adulthood, are factors they discuss in terms of their own lives and creativity."

351. ***Women and Creativity.*** 30 mins. Videocassette, color. 1982. Rental $55.00. Free preview. PBS Video.

A "technically well-produced program that poses the question of the compatibility of creativity and childrearing. Pictures by Mary Cassatt are shown as well as more traditional outlets for female creativity such as quilts and other handcrafts." Interviews with Judy Chicago discussing "Dinner Party," which features women's art expressed through crafts; with Benji, who creates sewn paintings and has chosen not to have children; and with "writer Mary Gordon about how she combines a career and motherhood."—*Catalyst* 2, no. 4: 9.

PERFORMING ARTS

352. ***Aretha Franklin, Soul Singer.*** 25 mins. 16 mm. film, color. 1969. Rental $33.00. McGraw-Hill Films.

Award-winning "close-up profile."

353. ***Jazz Women: A Feminist Retrospective.*** 2 records. Stash 109. $11.95. Ladyslipper.

Anthology of thirty-four performances, mostly of instrumental music (pianists Williams and Austin, guitarist Osborne, Liston on the trombone, Lil Armstrong Her Swing Band) with a few vocals from the 1920s to the early 1940s. "Feminist in that it focuses on women artists who became outstanding musicians in the face of all the obstacles . . . in the male-dominated jazz field." A classic.

354. ***Love It Like a Fool.*** 28 mins. 16 mm. film, color. Rental $45. New Day Films.

Award-winning documentary featuring Malvina Reynolds, songwriter, folksinger, and activist, who, in her seventies, talks about age, relationships, her concern with social change, her art, and shares some of her life, private and public, with her audience.

355. ***Mean Mothers: Independent Women's Blues.*** Record. Rosetta 1300. $7.95. Ladyslipper.

"Refreshing anthology with good sound quality, which is difficult to obtain with reissues." Includes Brown's "Ain't Much Good in the Best of Men Nowadays" (1926), Cox's "One Hour Mama" (1939), and Holiday's "Baby Get Lost." Informative liner notes.

356. ***Red, White and Blues: Women Sing of America.*** Record. Rosetta 1302. $7.95. Ladyslipper.

Selected for "historical significance," women's blues and jazz songs on this album have a clean sound and are accompanied by informative notes. Includes Fitzgerald, Holiday, Smith, Spivey, and Bailey.

357. ***Woman's Work.*** 2 records. Gemini Hall 1010. $14.95. Ladyslipper.

Three centuries of classical works by European women composers. Various combinations of voice, strings, piano, and harpsichord, performed mostly by women, including the Vieuxtemps Quartet. Includes a forty-four-page *Booklet* of biographical notes.

358. ***Women of Old Time Music.*** Record. Heritage 36. $8.95. Ladyslipper.

Offers traditional music of women: lullabys, ballads, banjo, church piano, spirituals, and blues, all recorded live at the 1980 Brandywine Mountain Music Convention.

VISUAL ARTS

359. ***American Women Artists: The Colonial Period to 1900.*** 80 slides. By K. Petersen and M. Stofflet. $90.00. Harper & Row College Media.

Includes Native American and slave artists, colonial portraitists, and folk artists.

360. ***American Women Artists: The Twentieth Century.*** 80 slides. By K. Petersen and M. Stofflet. $90.00. Harper & Row College Media.

Social realism, mural painting, abstract expressionism, and nonobjective painting.

361. ***Anonymous Was a Woman.*** 30 mins. 16 mm. film/videocasette, color. 1980. Rental $25.50. University of Illinois.

Excerpts from letters, instruction manuals, and diaries counterpoint a stunning display of folk art (samplers, quilts, rugs, paintings, and needlework pictures) created by American women in the eighteenth and nineteenth centuries.

362. ***The Artist Was a Woman.*** 58 mins. 16 mm. film/videocassette, color. 1980. Rental $25.50. University of Illinois.

Filmed in major museums in Europe and America, this shows not only the works, often in detail, of some twenty artists in the course of a well-knit historical survey, but also "views of the towns and cities, the social [settings] and the studios where the artists lived and worked." Narration includes quotations from critics of the works, "facts about the careers and personal experiences of the artists, [and] excerpts from their diaries and letters." Interviews with the consultants—Harris, Nochlin, and Greer—deal with the issues of objectivity, feminist thought, and how "greatness" in art is decided.—*Women's Caucus for Art Newsletter* 10, no. 4. For five slide sets drawn from the film, see **363.**

363. ***The Artist Was a Woman: 1550–1950.*** 5 slide sets, about 40 per century. $28.00 per set. 1978. Budek Films and Slides.

A total of 185 color slides of 89 works by 36 artists varying in quality "from superb . . . to questionable," but "for the most part . . . very good." The "record of an impressive body of work that can easily be integrated into traditional art history courses," this collection covers only paintings, drawings, and prints, makes no reference to minority artists, and leaves out a number of major figures; but "by and large the best works by women . . . are well represented."—*Women's Caucus for Art Newsletter* 10, no. 4. Drawn from **362;** overlaps **369** by only thirteen slides.

364. ***Ethnic American Art Slide Library.*** Individual slides $1.20. The University of Southern Alabama.

Offers slides of works by the more than one hundred artists, about a quarter of them women, in the University's "Afro-American, American Indian, [and] Mexican American Collection." Free 134-page catalog, arranged by collection, lists slides under each artist's name, giving title of work, size, and genre.

365. ***Images—Themes and Dreams.*** 80 slides (mostly color). *Notes.* Part of a series by J. J. Wilson and K. Petersen. $90.00. Harper & Row College Media.

" 'Is there a uniquely female vision or imagery?' These slides look at women's sense of themselves and sources of imagery in creating art. The works are open to many interpretations. Some are quite terrifying, or have a satiric bite, while others joyously affirm the strength and originality of women as individuals." Includes Hohn, Toorop, Kahlo, Fini, Varo, Chicago, Wieland, and Edelson, among others. Notes and bibliography "explore ways in which women see themselves and each other through their art."

366. ***The Life and Death of Frida Kahlo.*** 40 mins. 16 mm. film, color. 1976. Rental $60.00. Serious Business.

Award-winning documentary concentrates on "the major events in her life: her crippling spinal injury, her tempestuous marriage to Diego Rivera, and above all, her dramatic exploration of personal obsessions in her painting."

367. ***Never Give Up: Imogene Cunningham.*** 28 mins. 16 mm. film, color. 1975. Rental $40.00. Phoenix Films.

Award-winning documentary records "an inspirational and intimate visit with the 92 year old portrait photographer."

368. ***The Originals: Women in Art.*** 30 mins. 16 mm. films/videocassettes, color. 1977. Rental $65.00 each. Films, Inc. (O'Keeffe is 60 mins., $95.00; Saar is $15.50 from University of Illinois.)

Biographical documentaries by award-winning producer "focus on the integration of each artist's life, the manner in which she works, and the influences that have inspired her particular style of creativity."

Georgia O'Keeffe "for the first time appears on camera" to talk about her work and life. Film includes rare home movie footage, comments by close friends and colleagues, and the scenes in New Mexico of her inspiration.

Nevelson in Process includes, for the first time, footage of the artist at work: "her 'process' is demonstrated as she creates two new sculptures, one of wood and one of metal."

Frankenthaler: Toward a New Climate has as its highlight "a remarkable sequence showing the actual creation of a painting from the mixing of the paint to the completion of the canvas."

Spirit Catcher—The Art of Betye Saar has the artist talking about the political messages of her work, and shows how in it "she liberates stereotyped black images from derogatory contexts while simultaneously creating old and new levels of awareness."

Mary Cassatt: Impressionist from Philadelphia shows examples of her work, and tells her personal story "through on-location footage, her art, contemporary documents, and voice-over dramatization based on her authentic memoirs."

Anonymous Was a Woman features folk art.

369. ***Women Artists: A Historical Survey (Early Middle Ages to 1900).*** 120 slides, mostly color. *Notes.* Part of a series by J. J. Wilson and K. Petersen. $120.00. Harper & Row College Media.

"Many unknown examples of women's art in the styles and periods most often examined in art history courses are faithfully reproduced." Both European and American artists are represented, among them Anguissola, Gentileschi, Kaufmann, Vigée-Lebrun, Bonheur, Cassatt, Morisot, and Valadon. Extensive notes examine both the lives of the artists and the historical perspectives of their paintings and sculpture. Includes a bibliography.

370. ***Women Artists: Photography.*** 80 slides. By K. Petersen and M. Stofflet. $99.00. Harper & Row College Media.

"Beginning with the remarkable portraits of Julia Margaret Cameron, this set goes on to trace the careers of many outstanding European and American women in portrait, documentary, pictorial and journalistic photography." Included, among others, are Käsebier, Beals, Cunningham, Lange, Jacobi, Modotti, Abbott, Freund, Arbus, and Dater.

371. ***Women Artists: Sculpture.*** 80 slides. *Notes.* By K. Petersen and M. Stofflet. $99.00. Harper & Row College Media.

Spans the nineteenth and twentieth centuries, and "ranges from portrait medals designed by Laure Fraser and three-dimensional social realist works of Abastenia St. Leger Eberle to such monumental public sculptures as Adelaide Johnson's *Memorial to the Pioneers of the Women's Suffrage Movement* and the contemporary outdoor works of Louise Nevelson." Some others included are Hepworth, Richier, Chryssa, Oppenheim, Callery, Burke, Kazen, Dehner, and Falkenstein.

372. ***Women Artists: The Twentieth Century.*** 80 slides, mostly color. *Notes.* Part of a series by J. J. Wilson and K. Petersen. $90.00. Harper & Row College Media.

"Examines some of the most influential styles and genres of the twentieth century." Includes surrealists, Brooks, Munter, Kollwitz, Hepworth, Nevelson, Hesse, Krasner, and others. "The notes are biographic, critical and delightful, and include a valuable bibliography."

373. ***Women Artists: Third World.*** 80 slides, mostly color. *Notes.* Part of a series by J. J. Wilson and K. Petersen. $90.00. Harper & Row College Media.

The works included "respond to the individual and collective experiences of third-world American women." Some of the artists represented are Catlett, Savage, Amezcua, Velarde, Okubo, Ringgold, Saar, and Chase-Riboud. Notes "delineate the experiences, struggles and styles of the artists." Includes a bibliography.

— CROSS-CULTURAL STUDIES —

374. ***Amira's Choice.*** 20 mins. 16 mm. film, color. 1982. Order #56970. Rental $14.50. University of Illinois.

Dramatizes the struggle of a Druze girl torn between a tradition that prohibits women from seeking advanced education and her desire to be a doctor. Conveys the flavor of Druze culture, an independent rural offshoot of the Islamic faith spread throughout Syria, Lebanon, and Israel.

375. ***My Survival as an Aboriginal.*** 55 mins. 16 mm. film/videocassette, color. Rental $80.00. Serious Business.

The study of a culture in transition, this is the first film written and directed by an aboriginal woman. The film shows her people's dislocation and alienation, their fight for dignity, her own family's life under her matriarchal authority, and their continued relationship with the wilderness.

376. ***Women in a Changing World.*** 60 mins. 16 mm. film, color. 1975. Order #70090. Rental $20.00. University of Illinois.

Presents the status of women, and family planning attitudes, as women, neither privileged nor unusually disadvantaged, talk (with voice-over translations) about what is important in their lives. Filmed in Afghanistan, Hong Kong, Bolivia, Kenya, and the Soho Islands.

AFRICA

377. ***Amazulu—People of the Sky.*** 24 mins. 16 mm. film, color. 1979. Rental $14.50. Order #84411. University of Illinois.

Observes life among the Zulu in a typical village, with attention to the division of labor, folklore, and ritual. Accents the fact that much has remained unchanged in the lives of these people as far as gender roles are concerned.

378. ***Boran Women.*** 18 mins. 16 mm. film, color. 1974. Order #55168. Rental $10.50. University of Illinois.

Shows the daily lives of women in Northern Kenya, and how the availability of education and other aspects of modernization are changing women's attitudes even while they maintain their traditional and influential roles in a herding culture. Dialogue is in the native language.

379. ***Fear Woman.*** 28 mins. 16 mm. film, color. 1972. Order #83009. Rental $14.00. University of Illinois.

Delineates the status of women in the African nation of Ghana. Interviews with a Ghanian Supreme Court Judge, a village chief, and a businesswoman offer provocative comments on the social structure of Ghana, where women's economic power rivals men's and where political and social power is also rapidly becoming equal.

380. ***N!ai, the Story of a !Kung Woman.*** 59 mins. 16 mm. film/videocassette, color. Rental $65.00/$50.00. 1980. Documentary Educational Resources.

Award-winning portrayal of changes in this South African society over three decades. Footage from the 1950s shows some of the life N!ai recalls as a child: helping her mother collect roots and berries, the division of giraffe meat, her resistance to her own marriage at eight years of age. Later, her life on the government reservation includes the problems of money and secrecy, tuberculosis, and recruitment as fighters against guerilla forces.

381. ***Rivers of Sand.*** 83 mins. 16 mm. film, color. 1974. Rental $75.00. Phoenix Films.

The film attempts not only to portray the life of the Hamar of Ethiopia, who openly and indeed flamboyantly profess male supremacy as part of their traditional way of life, but also to show the effect on mood and behavior of a life governed by sexual inequality.

382. ***South Africa Belongs to Us.*** 35 mins. 16 mm. film, color. 1980. Rental $50.00. California Newsreel.

"It is accepted all over the world that women and their families be allowed to live with each other and build a life together"—but not if you are black in South Africa. An intimate portrait of the lives of five typical women who "face the cameras illegally to talk of their fear and frustration under apartheid. . . . All are eloquent."—*The Daily Mail.*

383. ***Traditional Women's Music from Ghana.*** Record. Folkways 4257. $9.95. Ladyslipper.

Includes songs from the Ewe, Fanti, Ashanti, Dagarti, and the Dagomba. Descriptive notes included.

384. ***West Africa: Two Life Styles.*** 18 mins. 16 mm. film, color. Rental $51.00. BFA Educational Media.

A comparison of the lives of a wealthy businesswoman in a modern African city and a yam farmer whose family is dependent on his crop, suggesting both striking contrasts and some similar cares and goals.

385. ***Women of the Toubou.*** 25 mins. 16 mm. film, color. 1974. Rental $40.00. Phoenix Films.

Truly nomadic, the Toubou of the Sahara are a strong matriarchy. Women are treated as equals by men, share every aspect of life, and are admired and respected as well as loved. This award-winning film shows the life of this people, who, while suffering from the severe drought in their region, resisted all earlier efforts by the French government, and now are resisting those of Chad, to control them.

386. ***You Have Struck a Rock!*** 20 mins. 16 mm. film, color. 1981. Rental $50.00. California Newsreel.

Their own stories told by South African women who took the lead in mobilizing mass opposition to apartheid during the anti-pass campaigns of the 1950s. Illustrated with historical footage, punctuated by South African music, and narrated by Letta Mbulu.

ASIA

387. ***An Anthology of Chinese Folksongs.*** Record. Folkways 8877. $8.95. Ladyslipper.

Songs are mostly in standard Chinese, with some local dialects. Includes a seven-page booklet with English notes on the songs and a glossary of Chinese terms.

388. ***Dadi's Family.*** 59 mins. 16 mm. film, color. Rental $50.00. Documentary Educational Resources.

This film explores an extended family in Northern India, and the problems of women: the tensions created by the authority of Dadi, who is both grandmother and mother-in-law; the loneliness of the veiled daughters-in-law, forever "outsiders"; and husbands' expectations. Also covered are social and economic changes that threaten the cohesion and stability of the family.

389. ***The Elusive Geisha.*** 26 mins. 16 mm. film, color. 1975. Order #83241. Rental $14.00. University of Illinois.

Shows geishas as entertainers with traditional music and dancing, their elaborate dressing rituals and daily activities, as it attempts to answer the question of why girls become geishas and what their place is in Japan's social structure.

390. ***Farm Song (The Japanese, Part 3).*** 59 mins. 16 mm. film, color. 1978. Order #90311. Rental $25.00. University of Illinois.

Introduces a family that owns ten acres of rice paddies three hundred miles from Tokyo and raises thoroughbreds for racing. Members of the four generations who live on the farm, which has been in the family for two hundred years, talk with an interviewer about family work and gender roles. Includes extensive scenes of family life.

391. ***Footbinding.*** 6 mins. 16 mm. film/videocassette, black and white. 1978. Rental $11.00. The Media Project.

A reenactment of the ancient footbinding ritual is combined with historical stills and contemporary documentary footage to provide a comprehensive view of the dynamics that force women to accept male-defined standards of beauty.

392. ***Old World, New Women.*** 28 mins. 16 mm. film, color. 1975. Order #84277. Rental $6.50. University of Illinois.

Presents a sampling of women who have become successful in their work in the Republic of China. A journalist, a television director, an architect, a politician, and members of a modern dance troupe are interviewed and observed.

393. ***Rana.*** 19 mins. 16 mm. film, color. 1976. Order #56245. Rental $13.00. University of Illinois.

Shows the world and life of Rana, a young Muslim woman in Old Delhi, India, and how she hovers between the traditional and modern.

LATIN AMERICA

394. ***Andean Women (The Aymara of the Bolivian Andes).*** 19 mins. 16 mm. film, color. 1974. Order #55343. Rental $10.50. University of Illinois.

Studies the role of women, who cook, spin, weave, work in the fields, and speak of their relationship with husbands and children. English subtitles.

395. ***Buenos Dias Compañeras: Women in Cuba.*** 57 mins. 16 mm. film, color. 1975. Order #70287. Rental $24.00. University of Illinois.

Women in all areas of Cuban life discuss (in Spanish with English translation) the equality they have achieved since the revolution. Shows women in nontraditional roles. Discussion covers changes in law, education, health care, and communal work; Castro, the Bay of Pigs, and much else.

396. ***The Double Day.*** 53 mins. 16 mm. film, color. Rental $75.00. Available in Spanish or English. Cinema Inc.

An accurate and comprehensive report on Latin American working-class women: peasants, miners, domestics, and market and factory workers. Filmed with sensitivity to caste, class, tradition, context, and feminism, it has fine photography, tight editing, and a good sound track that includes folk music and children's songs about work. The articulateness and even militancy of the women filmed counters the popular myth of the passive Latin American woman.

397. ***Jamaican Women.*** 29 mins. Videocassette, color. 1975. Rental $35.00. Free preview. Martha Stuart Communications.

Ten Jamaican women from all walks of life share their views and experiences on marriage, the subordinate position of women, and the instabilities of family life.

398. ***Simplemente Jenny.*** 33 mins. 16 mm. film, color. Rental $60.00. Available in Spanish or English. Cinema Inc.

Using old engravings, contemporary media images, and interviews with school children, teenage girls in a reformatory, slum women organizing, and others, the film explores the ideals and images shaping women's lives in Latin America today, and contrasts the models of society with the realities of poverty and violence.

ENGLISH

LANGUAGE AND COMMUNICATION

399. ***Killing Us Softly: Advertising's Image of Women.*** 30 mins. 16 mm. film, color. $46.00. Cambridge Documentary Films.

Presents a wide selection of advertisements accompanied by a witty and informative commentary, showing that advertising is a powerful form of cultural conditioning with a message that is deadly serious for women. An excellent discussion starter.

400. ***Sexism in Language and Media.*** 1 sound, 1 silent filmstrip. 35 activity posters. Worksheets. $57.00. Opportunities for Learning.

Explores the limited representation of males and females often found in media, and considers advertisements that exemplify both positive and negative aspects of sex roles. Encourages student evaluation of language for sexism.

LITERATURE

401. ***"And Ain't I a Woman?": 200 Years of Feminist Literature.*** 6 filmstrips, color. Cassettes/records. *Program Guide*. $33.00 each. Prentice-Hall Media.

Titled "Early Signs: 1642–1850," "Feminist Fifties," "Hearthside in the 1800's," "Outside (Late 1800's–Early 1900's)," "Society and Its Attitude," and "Towards a New Consciousness," these six filmstrips contrast the essays, prose, and poetry of women writers with the realities of women's lives. Featured are Adams, Fuller, Wollstonecraft, Stanton, the Grimkés, Truth, Anthony, Woolf, Lessing, Steinem, and others.

402. ***Ntozake Shange: For Colored Girls Who Have Considered Suicide.*** Record. $10.00. The Women's Audio Exchange.

Performance of Shange's successful Broadway show.

403. ***The Ordeal of the Woman Writer.*** Cassette. $12.00. The Women's Audio Exchange.

Jong, Morrison, and Piercy discuss their personal feelings about being writers and the problems they face.

404. ***The Poetry and Voice of*** **(Series).** Cassettes. $10.00–$12.00 each. The Women's Audio Exchange.

Angelou, Atwood, Kumin, Lifshin, Moore, Plath, Sexton, Stein, and Piercy read their poems. One cassette per author.

405. ***To Be a Woman and a Writer.*** 2 filmstrips. 2 cassettes. *Library Kit*. $79.00. The Center for Humanities.

Dramatic readings, literary analysis, and social background illustrate the emergence of women writers and their works, from Bradstreet to Hansberry.

406. ***Women in Literature.*** 4 filmstrips. 4 cassettes/records. $136.00. Educational Audio Visual.

Charts the transition of women in literature from object to subject, discussing authors from Homer and Virgil to Ibsen, Woolf, de Beauvoir, and Plath. Documentary visuals with text, which includes excerpts from works discussed. "Early Images" covers Greek myths, drama, and the Bible; "The Church and the Castle" covers medieval images up to Shakespeare; "The Proper Heroine" covers women novelists and early feminism; and "Changing Images" covers the contemporary scene.

407. ***Women in Literature.*** Cassettes. $12.00 each. Everett Edwards.

Wide range of titles, from *Women in Medieval Literature* (Joan Ferrante), to *Women in Milton* (Joan Hartman), in *Shakespeare,* 5 titles (Margaret Ronald), *Yeats* and *Eliot* (Carol Smith), *American Literature* (Wendy Martin), *Dostoyevsky* (Deborah Fort), *Faulkner* (Martha Nochinson), and *Women as Literary Innovators* (Grace Schulman). Also individual woman writers, including *Sand, Stein, Dickinson, Hellman, Oates, Lessing, Plath, Piercy, Wakoski,* and more.

408. ***Women in Literature Reading Their Own Works.*** Cassettes. Set of 6. $50.00. Caedmon.

Includes Brooks, Moore, Porter, Sitwell, Stein, and Welty.

409. ***The Writer in America* (Series).** 29 mins. 16 mm. film, color. 1975–78. $16.50. University of Illinois.

Interviews with authors who also read from their own works. Available: *Eudora Welty* (Order #84422), *Janet Flanner* (#84418), *Muriel Rukeyser* (#84421), *Toni Morrison* (#84420).

HISTORY

UNITED STATES HISTORY

410. ***The American Woman: A Social Chronicle.*** 6 filmstrips, color. 6 cassettes. $141.00. Social Studies School Service.

Chronological format includes "Puritans and Patriots," "'Mill Girls,' Intellectuals and the Southern Myth," "Pioneer Women and the Belles of the Wild West," "The Suffragist, the Working Woman, the Flapper," "Breadlines, Assembly Lines, Togetherness," and "Liberation Now!" The *Teacher's Guide* includes a listing of notable American women 1607–1950, by profession.

411. ***The American Woman: Portraits of Courage.*** 53 mins. 16 mm. film/videocassette, color. 1976. Rental $25.00. University of Illinois.

Multiple-award-winning drama-documentary highlights the careers of ten women: fighters in the American Revolution, suffragists, groundbreakers in the professions, social workers, labor organizers, and civil rights workers. Includes archival illustrations, early film footage, interviews, and actors' research-based recreations of characters, from the eighteenth century to the present. Deals with both notable and anonymous women. Includes *Guide* with discussion questions, projects, and bibliography.

412. ***American Women.*** 6 filmstrips, color. 6 cassettes. 15 mins. each. 1980. $115.00. Free preview. Coronet Media.

"Poor photographic quality, intrusive music. . . . Sequences are unrelated . . . the overall effect is not informative or interesting."—*Catalyst* 1, no. 1.

413. ***The Changing Role of Women.*** 2 filmstrips, color. 2 cassettes/records. $69.00. Prentice-Hall Media.

"The historic struggle of women in seeking to overcome their stereotyped image is reviewed." Also, "the impact of modern women on the world of today and of the future" is examined. Includes a *Program Guide*.

414. ***The Emerging Woman.*** 40 mins. 16 mm. film, black and white. Rental $50.00. Cinema Inc.

A carefully researched, award-winning documentary that uses old engravings, photos, and newsreels to show the varied economic, social, and cultural experiences of women from 1800 on. Topics dealt with include mill girls and early labor organizing; black, immigrant, and upper-class women in Victorian society; the abolitionist and suffrage movements; the myth of the flapper and media-created images; and the feminine mystique, civil rights, and women's liberation. Attractive seventeen-page *Study/Activity Booklet* provides sound background information and some thoughtful and easy-to-use teaching suggestions.

415. ***The Woman's Role: America and England.*** **(Part of *The American Revolution: Who Was Right?* series.)** Filmstrip, color. 2 cassettes. $33.00. Opportunities for Learning.

Both sides of the issues are revealed through images and dialogue. One cassette gives the English, the other the American interpretation of the same event. *Discussion Guide* included.

416. ***Women: An American History.*** 6 sound filmstrips. 17 mins. each. $27.00 each/$146 for all. Encyclopedia Britannica Educational Corporation.

Award-winning filmstrip series examines the social, economic, educational, and political changes that have affected women's role, and highlights outstanding women. Strips encompass "Women of the New World," "The Mill Girl and the Lady," "The Fight for Equality," "A Combination of Work and Hope," "Beyond the Vote," and "The Modern Women's Movement." *Discussion Guide* included.

417. ***Women in American History.*** 6 sound filmstrips, color. 3 cassettes. $92.00. Educational Activities.

Award-winning series presents "memorable vignettes from the lives of outstanding women and brief excerpts from their speeches and writings." Includes "The Colonies" (Hutchinson, witch trials, Brent, Adams), "After the Revolution" (pioneers, industrial revolution, slave and factory women, Southern life), "Slavery and Suffrage" (abolitionist leaders, Seneca Falls, Anthony, Mott, Stone, the

Civil War), "Reformers" (immigrants, Hull House, sweatshops, the Women's Trade Union League, Jones), "Crisis of Identity" (discrimination in education, employment, law, media, Roosevelt, Friedan, Chisholm), and "The Artist" (Lange, Graham, Nevelson, St. Marie, Brooks). Includes a *Manual* with projects and worksheets.

418. ***Women in the American Revolution.*** 2 filmstrips. Record/cassette. $30.00. Multi-Media Productions.

419. ***Women in the Civil War.*** Filmstrip. Cassette. $25.00. Multi-Media Productions.

EUROPEAN HISTORY

420. ***Donna: Women in Revolt.*** 65 mins. 16 mm. film, color. 1980. Rental $115.00. Iris Films.

Shows the effects of political and social policies on the daily lives of Italian women, and how they have responded, as it tells the story of the Italian women's movement from 1900 to the present. Uses newsreel clips, montage, and interviews to cover women in the early farmers' and workers' movements, feminism, women and fascism, the resistance movement of World War II, and how feminists pushed successfully for abortion and divorce laws in the 1970s.

421. ***Women in Ancient History.*** Individual cassettes. $12.00 each. Everett Edwards.

"Women in Bronze Age Greece," by Sarah Pomeroy. "Women in Sparta and Athens," by Sarah Pomeroy. "Women in Ancient Rome," by Daniel Coogan.

422. ***Women in Modern European History.*** Individual cassettes. $12.00 each. Everett Edwards.

"Early European Feminists," by Susan Bell. "Christine de Pisan," by Diane Bornstein. "Mme. de Stael," by Susan Tenenbaum. "Mary Wollstonecraft," by Marcelle Thiebaux.

SCIENCE

423. ***Sandra, Zella, Dee and Claire: Four Women in Science.*** 17 mins. 16 mm. film/videocassette, color. 1978. $8.00/$5.00. Education Development Center.

An astronomer, a laser physicist, a veterinarian, and a mechanical engineer are interviewed. They comment on their work, educational preparation, job satisfaction, and personal lifestyles (one is a two-career family member with two small children).

424. ***A Woman's Place: Biology and Destiny.*** Filmstrip. Cassette/record. *Program Guide*. $33.00. Prentice-Hall Media.

Presents contrasting views by Freud, Money, and others on whether women's biological processes and hormonal structure should determine their socioeconomic roles, and discusses sex identity and sex-role socialization.

SOCIAL SCIENCE

THE FAMILY

425. ***Children of Working Mothers.*** 29 mins. 16 mm. film/videocassette, color. *Discussion Guide*. 1979. Rental $50.00/$35.00. Martha Stuart Communications.

Children, aged ten to eighteen, of working mothers from rural, suburban, and urban environments, talk of how it feels to come home to an empty house, the special ways they spend time with their mothers, and their sense of pride in their mothers' work.

426. ***Joyce at 34.*** 28 mins. 16 mm. film, color. Rental $40.00. New Day Films.

A case study of a woman who faces the conflict between work and family, this award-winning documentary explores the first year of motherhood for filmmaker Joyce Chopra. A very personal statement in an atypical context (the husband is a writer), which nevertheless raises important issues.

427. ***Single Parents.*** 28 mins. 16 mm. film/videocassette, color. 1980. Rental $35.00/$50.00. Free preview. Martha Stuart Communications.

The women and men in this program have come to single parenthood as a result of divorce, death, adoption, or birth without a husband. They discuss their open, sharing relationships with their children; fathers talk about sex-role stereotyping and how they had to get in touch with their feminine side; the differences between being a male and a female single parent; and relationships with step-parents or unmarried partners. The emphasis is positive, constructive, and supportive.

428. ***Today's Family: A Changing Concept.*** Filmstrip, color. Cassette. *Guide*. $27.50. Current Affairs.

Analyzes the social and personal effects of changes in the concept and function of the family, from the extended family of nineteenth-century America to the nuclear and one-parent families of more recent years.

RAPE

429. ***No Exceptions.*** 24 mins. 16 mm. film, color. 1977. Order #83957. Rental $15.00. University of Illinois.

Deals with rape prevention, what to do if rape occurs, and the steps to be taken afterwards.

430. ***Rape: A Preventive Inquiry.*** 18 mins. 16 mm. film, color. 1974. Order #54608. Rental $12.50. Available in Spanish. University of Illinois.

Award-winning film presents three case histories of rape attacks from the victims' point of view, contrasted with four convicted rapists' perspectives. Police investigators show how to avoid potential rape situations, and discuss methods of escape and survival alternatives.

431. ***Rape Culture.*** 35 mins. 16 mm. film, color. Rental $46.00. Cambridge Documentary Films.

Examines popular films, advertising, music, and "adult entertainment," establishing the connections between violence and "normal" patterns of male-female behavior. It presents statistics and the ideas of many concerned about rape, including rape crisis center workers, authors Mary Daly and Emily Culpepper, and a convicted multiple rapist now released from prison.

432. ***The Rape Victims.*** 24 mins. 16 mm. film, color. 1978. Order #84154. Rental $15.00. University of Illinois.

Documentary narrated by a victim shows why, when, how, and to whom rape happens, explains why so many rapes go unreported, and offers advice on how to avoid being raped.

433. ***The Trouble with Rape.*** 28 mins. 16 mm. film, color. 1975. Rental $15.75. Order #83670. University of Illinois.

Interviews three women of varying ages and stations in life, to illustrate that rape can happen to anyone. Reveals how the double standard and myths about rape leave the woman without support, even when her assailant pleads guilty.

GENDER ROLES

434. ***Growing Up Female.*** 50 mins. 16 mm. film/videocassette, black and white. Rental $40.00. New Day Films.

Shows the socialization of the American woman through a personal look into the lives of six females, aged four to thirty-five, including the forces that shape them: parents, teachers, guidance counselors, advertising images, pop music, and the institution of marriage.

435. ***Male/Female: Changing Lifestyles.*** 4 filmstrips. 4 cassettes/records. $136.00. Educational Audio Visual.

Theories of sex-role differentiation, social expectations and prohibitions, anatomical differences, and analogies with animal behavior are explored in a format that includes discussions among children, teens, and adults, documentary visuals, and a correlated narration. Presented in three units—"Biology and Behavior: The Old Traditions," which examines sex roles in historical context, covering early women's movements, World War I, and the vote; "The Feminine Mystique"; and "Modern Trends," which details the impact of the new feminism on both women and men, and discusses alternative lifestyles, changes in family life, and points at issue in the movement.

436. ***Masculinity.*** 4 filmstrips, color. 4 cassettes/records. *Program Guides.* $33.00 each. Prentice-Hall Media.

"What Is a Man?" provides biological, cultural, and comparative perspectives; "The Masculine Image" explores the attributes ascribed to men in American history, the roles and stereotypes, and the effects these have had; "Manhood" deals with the special problems of black men and their identity in poems by Hughes, Ledbetter, Evans, and others; "What Makes a Man?" examines, through a case history, the difficulties many men have today in working out problems of self-image, identity, lifestyle, and personal values.

437. ***Men under Siege: Life with the Modern Woman.*** 33 mins. 16 mm. film/videocassette, color. $470.00/$300.00. ABC Wide World of Learning.

A documentary with insight and humor, this shows the experiences of men who work for women, and who take greater responsibility for children and household tasks. A wide range of feelings about work, sexual relations, family, and marriage is revealed that unmasks stereotypes and shows new possibilities for the future.

438. ***Men's Lives.*** 43 mins. 16 mm. film/videocassette, color. Rental $58.00. New Day Films.

Academy Award-winning documentary combines movie clips, interviews with high school teachers, the reflections of media heroes, and frank conversations with men and boys. It offers insight into the conditioning, attitudes, and experiences of men in contemporary America.

439. ***New Relationships for Men and Women.*** 2 slide sets, each with 160 slides. 2 cassettes/records. $169.00 each/$305.10 for both. The Center for Humanities.

Unit One—"Man and Woman: Myths and Stereotypes." Explores the models presented in literature, movies, media, and songs, and their effects on adult relationships.

Unit Two—"The Re-education of Women and Men: Creating New Relationships." Students' responses to the material presented are intended to lead to an awareness of their own attitudes and an evaluation of both the latter and of the stereotypes in light of objective data. Changes in traditional male-female relationships are also explored.

440. ***Sex Role Development.*** 23 mins. 16 mm. film/videocassette, color. Rental $39.00. McGraw-Hill Films.

Examines the influence sex roles and stereotypes have on almost every facet of people's lives, the ways in which those roles and stereotypes are instilled, and the search for better models of human behavior.

441. ***Superman and the Bride.*** 42 mins. 16 mm. film, color. 1975. Order #90307. Rental $20.00. University of Illinois.

Uses still photographs, animation, and film clips (some include nudity) to show how mass media perpetuate stereotypical gender roles, and suggests how this perpetuation benefits the media. Examples from China and Sweden show how stereotypes are being broken.

442. ***Three Domestics.*** 36 mins. 16 mm. film, black and white. Rental $45.00. Documentary Educational Resources.

Shows Pittsburgh police intervening in three domestic situations: a woman in a black household asks police to remove the man she has been living with in common law, for assaulting her; a woman accuses her boyfriend of beating her, and the man accuses her of lying; and a drunken father is taken to jail at the insistence of his wife and older son.

443. ***To Be a Man: The Other Side of Women's Liberation.*** 44 mins. 16 mm. film/videocassette, color. $629.00/$377.00. Perspective Films and Video.

Award-winning "discussion-starter" asks and answers questions about the rightness of the view that man should be breadwinner, provider, doer, and representative of the family to the world. Introduces men who chose to be individuals rather than follow stereotypes.

444. ***Who You Are and What You Are: Understanding Sex Roles.*** 4 filmstrips, color. 4 cassettes. Videocassette, 41 mins. *Guide*. 1982. $149.50. The Center for Humanities.

Helps to create an understanding of how historical, social, and cultural conditions have influenced the formation of gender roles; presents examples of individuals grappling with specific problems; and emphasizes the need for individuals to find lifestyles that suit their own talents and wants in the areas of jobs, marriage partners, sexuality, and relationships.

445. ***Women Like Us.*** 52 mins. 16 mm. film/videocassette, color. 1979. Rental (film only) $65.00. Free preview. Films, Inc.

In-depth profile of three women happy with the lifestyles they have chosen: a working wife and mother, a top executive who wishes to remain single and childless, and a homemaker.

DIRECTORY OF PUBLISHERS AND DISTRIBUTORS

Note: Addresses for periodicals are included here under the title of the periodical.

ABC Wide World of Learning Inc.
1330 Ave. of the Americas
New York, NY 10019

ABC-Clio
Box 4397, 2040 Alameda Padre Serra
Santa Barbara, CA 93140

Addison-Wesley Publishing Co., Inc.
One Jacob Way
Reading, MA 01867

Alyson Publications
Box 2783
Boston, MA 02208

American Historical Association
400 A St. SE
Washington, DC 20003

American Historical Review
914 Atwater
Bloomington, IN 47405

American Sociological Association
Teaching Resources Center
1722 N St. NW
Washington, DC 20036

Anchor/Doubleday
See: Doubleday Publishing Co.

Antelope Island Press
Box 220
St. George, UT 84770

Avon Books
1790 Broadway
New York, NY 10019

Ayer Co.
47 Pelham Rd.
Salem, NH 03079

Bantam Books Inc.
666 Fifth Ave.
New York, NY 10103

Basic Books Inc.
10 E. 53 St.
New York, NY 10022

Beacon Press
25 Beacon St.
Boston, MA 02108

BFA Educational Media
468 Park Ave. S.
New York, NY 10016

Biblio Press
Box 22
Fresh Meadows, NY 11365

B'nai B'rith Anti-Defamation League
823 United Nations Plaza
New York, NY 10017

The Bobbs-Merrill Co., Inc.
Box 558, 4300 W. 62 St.
Indianapolis, IN 46206

Budek Films and Slides
73 Pelham St.
Newport, RI 02840

Caedmon
1995 Broadway
New York, NY 10023

California Newsreel
630 Natoma St.
San Francisco, CA 94103

Cambridge Documentary Films, Inc.
Box 385
Cambridge, MA 02139

Cambridge University Press
32 E. 57th St.
New York, NY 10022

Carousel Films, Inc.
241 E. 34th St., Room 304
New York, NY 10016

Catalyst Media Review
Catalyst National Headquarters
250 Park Ave. S.
New York, NY 10003

The Center for Humanities
Communications Park, Box 1000
Mount Kisco, NY 10549

Center for Teaching International Relations
University of Denver
Denver, CO 80208

The Cinema Guild
1697 Broadway
New York, NY 10019

Cinema Inc.
Box 315
Franklin Lakes, NJ 07417

Clarity Educational Productions Inc.
4560 Horton St.
Emeryville, CA 94608

Collector Records
1604 Arbor View Rd.
Silver Springs, MD 20902

Collier Macmillan International
866 Third Ave.
New York, NY 10022

The Common Women Collective
c/o Women's Center
46 Pleasant St.
Cambridge, MA 02139

Consortium for Educational Equity
Rutgers University
Kilmer Campus 4090
New Brunswick, NJ 08903

Coronet Media
65 E. S. Water St.
Chicago, IL 60601

Creative Learning Inc.
3201 New Mexico Ave.
Washington, DC 20016

Crown Publishers Inc.
225 Park Ave. S.
New York, NY 10003

Current Affairs
Box 426
346 Ethan Allen Hwy. (Rte. 7)
Ridgefield, CT 06877

Diemer-Smith
3377 Solano, Suite 322
Napa, CA 94558

Documentary Educational Resources
5 Bridge St.
Watertown, MA 02172

Doubleday Publishing Co.
245 Park Ave.
New York, NY 10167

Drama Book Publishers
821 Broadway
New York, NY 10003

Education Development Center
55 Chapel St.
Newton, MA 02160

Educational Activities Inc.
Box 392
Freeport, NY 11520

Educational Audio Visual Inc.
Pleasantville, NY 10570

Educational Equity Concepts, Inc.
440 Park Ave. S.
New York, NY 10016

Everett Edwards Inc.
Box 1060
Deland, FL 32720

Encyclopedia Britannica Educational
Corp.
425 N. Michigan Ave.
Chicago, IL 60611

Farrar Straus Giroux Inc.
19 Union Sq. W.
New York, NY 10003

The Feminist Press at The City
University of New York
311 E. 94 St.
New York, NY 10128

Feminist Studies
c/o The Women's Studies Program
University of Maryland
College Park, MD 20742

Films, Inc.
1213 Wilmette Ave.
Wilmette, IL 60091

Ford Foundation
320 E. 43 St.
New York, NY 10017

Frontiers
Women Studies Program
Box 35, University of Colorado
Boulder, CO 80309

Gale Research Co.
Book Tower
Detroit, MI 48226

Gordian Press Inc.
Box 304, 85 Tompkins St.
Staten Island, NY 10304

Greenwood Press
Box 5007, 88 Post Rd. W.
Westport, CT 06881

Hackett Publishing Co. Inc.
Box 44937
Indianapolis, IN 46204

G. K. Hall and Co.
70 Lincoln St.
Boston, MA 02111

Harcourt Brace Jovanovich
1250 Sixth Ave.
San Diego, CA 92101

Harper & Row College Media
2350 Virginia Ave.
Hagerstown, MD 21740

Harper & Row, Publishers Inc.
10 E. 53 St.
New York, NY 10022

Harper & Row San Francisco
1700 Montgomery St.
San Francisco, CA 94111

Harvard Educational Review
Longfellow Hall
13 Appian Way
Cambridge, MA 02138

Harvard University Press
79 Garden St.
Cambridge, MA 02138

D. C. Heath and Co.
125 Spring St.
Lexington, MA 02173

Helaine Victoria Press, Inc.
4080 Dynasty Lane
Martinsville, IN 46151

Hill and Wang
19 Union Sq. W.
New York, NY 10003

The History Teacher
Department of History
6101 E. 7 St.
California State University
Long Beach, CA 90840

Holmes and Meier Publishers Inc.
IUB Building
30 Irving Pl.
New York, NY 10003

Holt, Rinehart and Winston
521 Fifth Ave., Sixth Floor
New York, NY 10175

Houghton Mifflin
One Beacon St.
Boston, MA 02108

Indiana University Press
Tenth and Morton Sts.
Bloomington, IN 47405

Information Systems Development
1100 E. Eighth
Austin, TX 78702

Intercultural Press Inc.
Box 768
Yarmouth, ME 04096

Interfaith Center on Corporate
Responsibility
475 Riverside Dr.
New York, NY 10027

Iris Films
Box 5353
Berkeley, CA 94704

Johns Hopkins University Press
Baltimore, MD 21211

Journal of Family History
JAI Press
36 Sherwood Pl., Box 1678
Greenwich, CT 06836

Journal of Interdisciplinary History
28 Carleton St.
Cambridge, MA 02142

Kendall-Hunt Publishing Co.
2460 Kerper Blvd.
Dubuque, IA 52001

Alfred A. Knopf Inc.
201 E. 50 St.
New York, NY 10022

Know Inc.
Box 86031
Pittsburgh, PA 15221

Ladyslipper, Inc.
Box 3124
Durham, NC 27705

Lawrence Hall of Science
Attn.: EQUALS
University of California
Berkeley, CA 94720

Legacy Books
Box 494
Hatboro, PA 19040

Libraries Unlimited Inc.
Box 263
Littleton, CO 80160

Light-Saraf Films
131 Concord St.
San Francisco, CA 94112

Little, Brown and Co., Inc.
34 Beacon St.
Boston, MA 02106

Longman Inc.
1560 Broadway
New York, NY 10036

Macmillan Publishing Co.
866 Third Ave.
New York, NY 10022

Gary E. McCuen
Gem Publications
411 Mallalieu Dr.
Hudson, WI 54016

McFarland and Co., Inc., Publishers
Box 611
Jefferson, NC 28640

McGraw-Hill Films
Del Mar, CA 92014

McGraw-Hill Inc.
1221 Ave. of the Americas
New York, NY 10020

Mayfield Publishing Co.
285 Hamilton Ave.
Palo Alto, CA 94301

The Media Project
Box 4093
Portland, OR 97208

MIT Press
28 Carleton St.
Cambridge, MA 02142

Monthly Review Press
155 W. 23 St.
New York, NY 10001

William Morrow and Co., Inc.
105 Madison Ave.
New York, NY 10016

Multi-Media Productions Inc.
Box 5097
Stanford, CA 94305

National Council for the Social Studies
3615 Wisconsin Ave. NW
Washington, DC 20016

National Council of Teachers of English
1111 Kenyon Rd.
Urbana, IL 61801

National Education Association
1201 16 St. NW
Washington, DC 20036

National Women's History Week Project
Box 3716
Santa Rosa, CA 95402

New American Library
1633 Broadway
New York, NY 10019

New Day Films
Box 315
Franklin Lakes, NJ 07417

New Society Publishers
4722 Baltimore Ave.
Philadelphia, PA 19143

Newbury House Publishers Inc.
54 Warehouse Lane
Rowley, MA 01969

W. W. Norton & Co.
500 Fifth Ave.
New York, NY 10110

On Campus With Women
Association of American Colleges
1818 R St. NW
Washington, DC 20009

Opportunities for Learning, Inc.
8950 Lurline Ave., Dept. X9
Chatsworth, CA 91311

Oxford University Press Inc.
200 Madison Ave.
New York, NY 10016

Pantheon Books Inc.
201 E. 50 St.
New York, NY 10022

PBS Video
475 L'Enfant Plaza SW
Washington, DC 20024

Penguin Books
40 W. 23 St.
New York, NY 10010

The Pennsylvania State University Press
215 Wagner Bldg.
University Park, PA 16802

Pergamon Press Inc.
Maxwell House, Fairview Park
Elmsford, NY 10523

Perspective Films and Video
65 E. S. Water St.
Chicago, IL 60601

Phoenix Films Inc.
470 Park Ave. S.
New York, NY 10016

Praeger Publishers
521 Fifth Ave.
New York, NY 10175

Prentice-Hall Inc.
Englewood Cliffs, NJ 08865

Prentice-Hall Media
150 White Plains Rd.
Tarrytown, NY 10591

Princeton University Press
Princeton, NJ 08540

The Putnam Publishing Group, Inc.
200 Madison Ave.
New York, NY 10016

Rand McNally & Co.
Box 7600
Chicago, IL 60680

Random House Inc.
201 E. 50 St.
New York, NY 10022

Resources for Feminist Research
Ontario Institute for Studies in
Education
252 Blour St. W.
Toronto, Ontario M5S 1V6
CANADA

Routledge and Kegan Paul
9 Park St.
Boston, MA 02108

St. Martin's Press Inc.
175 Fifth Ave.
New York, NY 10010

Scarecrow Press
52 Liberty St.
Metuchen, NJ 08840

Schenkman Books Ltd.
190 Concord Ave.
Cambridge, MA 02138

Schocken Books Inc.
62 Cooper Sq.
New York, NY 10003

Abner Schram Ltd.
36 Park St.
Montclair, NJ 07042

Science Research Associates
155 N. Wacker
Chicago, IL 60606

Serious Business
1145 Mandana Blvd.
Oakland, CA 04610

M. E. Sharpe Inc.
80 Business Park Dr.
Armonk, NY 10504

Shenandoah Film Productions
538 G St.
Arcata, GA 95531

The Shoe String Press Inc.
Box 4327, 995 Sherman Ave.
Hamden, CT 06514

Signs
See: University of Chicago Press

Simon & Schuster Inc.
1230 Ave. of the Americas
New York, NY 10020

Social Education
3501 Newark St. NW
Washington, DC 20016

Social Studies School Service
10000 Culver Blvd., Dept. 13
Culver City, CA 90230

Stanford University Press
Stanford, CA 94305

State University of New York Press
State University Plaza
Albany, NY 12246

Martha Stuart Communications Inc.
Box 127, 2 Anthony St.
Hillsdale, NY 12529

TABS
744 Carroll St.
Brooklyn, NY 11215

Teachers College Press
Teachers College, Columbia University
1234 Amsterdam Ave.
New York, NY 10027

Temple University Press
Broad and Oxford Sts.
Philadelphia, PA 19122

Transaction Books
Rutgers University
New Brunswick, NJ 08903

Twayne Publishers
70 Lincoln St.
Boston, MA 02111

United Nations
Development Education Center
UNICEF Office for Europe
Palais des Nations CH-1211
Geneva 10
SWITZERLAND

United States Commission on Civil Rights
Distribution Center
621 N. Payne St.
Alexandria, VA 22314

United States Government Printing Office
Superintendent of Documents
Washington, DC 20402

University of California Institute of International Studies
215 Moses Hall
Berkeley, CA 94720

University of California Press
2120 Berkeley Way
Berkeley, CA 94720

University of Chicago Press
5801 Ellis Ave.
Chicago, IL 60637

University of Illinois
Film Center
1325 S. Oak St.
Champaign, IL 61820

University of Illinois Press
54 E. Gregory Dr.
Champaign, IL 61820

The University of Michigan Press
Box 1104, 839 Greene St.
Ann Arbor, MI 48106

University of Nebraska Press
901 N. 17 St.
Lincoln, NE 68588

University of New Mexico Press
Journalism Bldg.
Albuquerque, NM 87131

The University of North Carolina Press
Box 2288
Chapel Hill, NC 27514

The University of Southern Alabama
College of Arts and Sciences
Ethnic American Art Slide Library
Mobile, AL 36688

University of Texas Press
Box 7819
Austin, TX 78713

University of Toronto Press
33 E. Tupper St.
Buffalo, NY 14203

University of Wisconsin Press
114 N. Murray St.
Madison, WI 53715

The University of Wisconsin System
112A Memorial Library
728 State St.
Madison, WI 53706

Watson-Guptill Publications
1515 Broadway
New York, NY 10036

West Publishing Co.
Box 3526, 50 W. Kellogg Blvd.
St. Paul, MN 55166

Women and Literature Collective
Box 441
Cambridge, MA 02138

Women Make Movies
19 W. 21 St.
New York, NY 10010

Women Studies Abstracts
Rush Publishing
Box 1
Rush, NY 14543

The Women's Audio Exchange
Box 273
Cambridge, NY 12816

Women's Institute for Freedom of the Press
3306 Ross Pl. NW
Washington, DC 20008

Women's Studies Quarterly
See: The Feminist Press at The City University of New York

Worldwatch Institute
1776 Massachusetts Ave. NW
Washington, DC 20036

Yale University Press
302 Temple St.
New Haven, CT 06520

AUTHOR/TITLE INDEX

PRINT RESOURCES

NOTE: Numerals refer to entry numbers, not page numbers.

AUDIOVISUAL RESOURCES

SUBJECT INDEX

NOTE: Entries that provide in-depth treatment of a subject are indicated in boldface type.